Marcelle Fauch

Three Months
with the English

A Tale of the Battle of Normandy, June-August 1944

OREP

EDITIONS

Note to the reader:

The texts taken from Marcelle Fauchier Delavigne's diary are translated as faithfully as possible to their handwritten and/or machine-typed (depending on the version) originals. The edited version appears in roman, while the handwritten, blue and machine-typed versions appear in italics. Texts with larger margins offer Claudie Fauchier Delavigne's clarifications. The author's choice of the word 'English', rather than 'British' or 'Allied', reflects knowledge and usage at the time.

PREFACE

June 1944. Marcelle Fauchier Delavigne lived opposite the Saint-Gabriel Priory, where around forty boys studied and boarded at the garden Centre she helped create with her husband, Emmanuel, in 1929.

From this vantage point, she observed the first few weeks of the liberation of France, keeping a day-to-day diary written with a pencil on small sheets of paper.

The diary begins on June 4th and continues until her husband's arrival in Paris on August 27th, where he was forced to remain due to the ongoing battles in Calvados. Written in short sentences, it takes us to the very heart of events, the village's liberation, the integration of the British troops, both in her home and in the priory, and her commitment as a translator in British material supply camps.

In the months that followed the end of the war, Marcelle Fauchier Delavigne, who was also a woman of letters, wrote a text from these notes taken on the spot, which was later published by the *La Renaissance du Bessin* press. This text, reduced to around twenty pages due to paper shortages, was the result of a first draft in blue ink, then a second in black ink, and two machine-typed texts.

This book includes all the aforementioned and complementary versions, together with selected comments, pictures and maps.

Claudie Fauchier Delavigne,
President of the Cultural Association of the Saint-Gabriel Priory

BIOGRAPHY

Marcelle Delavigne was born on April 20th 1883 in the 9th *arrondissement* of Paris, and was baptised in the nearby church of Saint-Louis-d'Antin.

She was the third daughter of Arthur Delavigne and Emma Worms[1], and, up to 1923, she lived in a building on Boulevard Haussmann, the lower floors of which housed the offices of a shipping company and a bank.

La Casa d'Arlequin, located on the top floor of the building, was a large room with a stage where small theatrical performances were given before an audience of friends from the worlds of business and culture. Indeed, Marcelle's father, Arthur Delavigne, was the son of the playwright Germain Delavigne, whose name fell into oblivion even more than that of his brother, Casimir Delavigne. Germain Delavigne also wrote in collaboration with other authors, including Eugène Scribe, with whom his most notable production was the libretto for *La Muette de Portici* in 1828, with music composed by Daniel Auber.

Arthur Delavigne himself wrote short plays for the theatre in collaboration with Henri Meilhac and Jacques Normand. Marcelle Fauchier Delavigne was perfectly familiar with this atmosphere bathed in culture. She met with certain authors (Dumas) and musicians (Massenet), both in Paris and in Villers-sur-Mer, at the *Villa Marguerite*, acquired by her mother during her marriage to the military commander Franchetti, hero of the Franco-Prussian War.

---

1. See family tree on page 142.

After marrying Emmanuel Fauchier Magnan in 1904, she gave birth to two children, Colette (1906) and Jean (1915). In 1921, the couple moved to Paris, on the Left Bank of the Seine, near Boulevard Saint-Germain. At their housewarming party, a performance of *La fête chez Thérèse* was staged in a natural set by Georges Wague, in the presence of Reynaldo Hahn.

To preserve the 'Delavigne' name, which, otherwise, would have died out in the absence of direct male descendants, Emmanuel Fauchier Magnan obtained permission from the *Conseil d'État* (French Council of State) to change his name to Fauchier Delavigne (1908).

Marcelle Fauchier Delavigne naturally turned to writing, producing articles for periodicals and novels, under her own name and sometimes under the pseudonym Jenny Dorcelle. The family archives contain several unpublished texts.

In Paris, Marcelle and Emmanuel Fauchier Delavigne continued to mingle with figures from the world of art and literature. Marcelle Fauchier Delavigne's friends included a politician (Henri Caillavet), artists (Guy Arnoux, Georges Cain, Madrazo, Jacques-Émile Blanche), playwrights and actors (Henri Bernstein, Henri Lavedan, Charles Dullin and Marguerite Moreno), musicians (Gabriel Fauré), dancers (Serge Lifar), authors (Colette, Germaine Beaumont, Natalie Barney) and historians (Lenotre).

In 1914, Emmanuel Fauchier Delavigne, an industrialist, was called upon to run as a Radical candidate in Caen's 2nd constituency, winning 25% of votes. On that occasion, he invested in the purchase of the Saint-Gabriel Priory, an abandoned farm. After the war, he decided to establish a horticultural school for young boys and, in 1929, he opened France's first private garden Centre, after several years of conversion work.

From then on, the couple divided their time between Paris and Saint-Gabriel, where they lived in a house in front of the priory, the very house Marcelle Fauchier Delavigne lived in on D-Day.

A LITERARY TESTIMONY

Marcelle Fauchier Delavigne was used to keeping a diary. In her personal papers, we found the notes she took from Saturday, June 1st and Wednesday, August 7th, 1940, including her exodus, those from 1942 and those taken between June 4th and August 27th, 1944.

Marcelle Fauchier Delavigne undertook the complex task of rewriting these notes, taken on the spot, day after day, during the summer of 1944, very probably as early as the autumn of the same year, following the liberation of Normandy and Paris, to produce *Trois mois avec les Anglais* (*Three Months with the English*). The aim of this genuine literary work was to publish her account of the Battle of Normandy as seen from Saint-Gabriel and the surrounding area, from Bayeux to Creully. The 60-year-old writer preserved the structure and hybrid form of the original version, blurring the lines between first-person diary and an historical account. However, none of the original ten thousand or so words, handwritten on 24 numbered pages, were copied. Not one single day of her summer notes was left unchanged in the final version, be it in their order or their exact form. Over the course of the six drafts, revisions, erasures and modified passages are legion, and the final edited text is an astonishing combination of each of its intermediate stages. The result: even if the spontaneous, sometimes brief style, with its many nominal phrases (i.e., without verbs), is retained, the whole text becomes fluent and is enriched *a posteriori* by memories that were initially overlooked. Moreover, while the preliminary manuscripts covered all but one day of the period, twenty of them were deleted from the edited version, i.e., one day out of four. Finally, in June and August, several days were combined to form one single paragraph. When first published, the booklet from the *La Renaissance du Bessin* press comprised less than 30 pages, a limitation probably due to the post-war paper shortage. In no way does this diminish the value and pertinence of this sensitive and touching text.

'The air we breathe is no longer the same.' (June 7th)[2]. This sentence, already used in the blue version, is one of the most evocative in Marcelle Fauchier Delavigne's text, reflecting the author's concern to express the radical change of atmosphere brought about by the D-Day Landings and the progressive liberation of Normandy. Throughout her text, she constantly focuses on the passage of time and the weather over these tumultuous weeks. *'Overcast in the morning, better in the evening.'* (June 13th); *'A lot of wind all the time'* (June 14th); *'The sun rises against a red sky. How good it is!'* (June 15th); *'Very bad weather, dark, cold, strong wind.'* (June 21st); *'Very fine weather.'* (July 18th and August 1st); *'Very foggy in the morning.'* (August 5th) and so on. Most of the 85 days covered start or end with a reference to the weather (only fifteen or so omit it). As a sign of the importance that Marcelle Fauchier Delavigne attaches to these references, she hence enhances her text on the very first day of her story, that of the First Communion at Saint-Gabriel, on Sunday, June 4th absent from the original sheets, her reference to *'the weather was good'* appears in all following versions. The aim is undoubtedly to reinforce the unity of her text over the pages. Ultimately, this process shows Marcelle Fauchier Delavigne's sense of reality, as she insists on anchoring her story in the simplicity of everyday life. These repetitions give her text a specific rhythm of simplicity and spontaneity.

---

2. All dates are those of the final version.

Another repetitive feature is the reference to her mood. Neither pouring her heart out nor complaining, Marcelle Fauchier Delavigne often highlights the moments when she is exhausted or the days when she can take time to relax. '*Tonight I sleep a little despite the noise, I am so tired.*' (June 13th); '*Again a terrible night, little sleep.*' (June 18th); '*I bicycle home from Bayeux, unable to do more.*' (July 4th); '*Clearly, I cannot go on. I shall have a day's rest tomorrow.*' (July 21st); '*[...] my tiredness vanishes*' (July 29th); '*Rest all day in the sun beside the window, reading a little.*' (August 6th). Once again, Marcelle Fauchier Delavigne's narrative is simple, human, and close to her readers as if to further highlight the major upheavals and extraordinary events she witnesses.

Marcelle Fauchier Delavigne excels particularly in describing the changes in the landscape, the noises and people that surround her. There is first a lot of dust, then the surroundings look completely different. As early as June 6th, she notices that '*The road seems different from usual; it is as if time had stopped still.*' Two days later, she describes the Route de Fresnay as, '*white with dust, rutted, littered with guns, telegraph lines, with the posts knocked down, and unidentifiable murderous-looking and half-destroyed objects. An impression of disorder and ruin.*' (June 8th). On June 9th, she speaks of '*fog*', of a '*cloud*', on July 22nd, of a '*scourge*' on July 16th or of a '*curtain*' formed by the dust and mist (July 20th). Only a trip to the pasture behind the priory (July 29th) offers Marcelle Fauchier Delavigne a glimpse of some greenery.

The sounds that prevail are described as the '*great racket*' (June 6th), the '*terrible, astounding, constant*' noise. '*For the past three weeks we have known no silence*' (June 25th) and during the concert held on June 24th, '*The noise sometimes drowned the voice of the singers.*' Her own home is constantly shaken by the bombings, '*Loud guns tonight, the house shakes.*'

(July 17th). There are nevertheless some moments of calm and quiet that allow the narrator to reconnect with the sounds of nature, such as the toads trilling on two occasions, June 9th and 14th.

To resume, Marcelle Fauchier Delavigne writes, '*I have never so appreciated the value of silence.*' (June 28th). Marcelle Fauchier Delavigne is deeply affected by the ravages of war, '*The road is full of German cartridges, grenades, rifles, thrown down many of them broken, a complete picture of war.*' (June 7th). As the troops land, the passage of trucks seems like '*a torrent*' (June 9th) and, over time, contrary to expectations, the transformation intensifies, '*Everything is changed. On the road to La Délivrande, where it crosses the Courseulles road, a great crossing has been made, with a mound in the middle and an Eros on top. It is 'Piccadilly Circus'! An evocation of London... A little further, there is a graveyard of cars and other vehicles, a vast space covered with scrap-iron of the most extraordinary shapes...*' (July 30th). And it never seems to end, '*One meets them [the British soldiers] all along the roads, continually repairing the damage that is done again next day.*' (June 12th). New roads are being built, '*These enormous caterpillars that push a gigantic horizontal plough in front of them, immediately opening up new roads.*' (June 10th).

However, it is not all doom and gloom, and Marcelle Fauchier Delavigne does not fail to marvel at the rare but intense '*sight*' (the term appears three times in her writing) offered by the Allies' greatest achievements. On June 10th, after returning from Ver-sur-Mer, she writes, '*I have just seen the most beautiful spectacle in the world: under a threatening sky and hundreds of silver balloons, the whole British fleet covers the sea as far as the eye can see.*' She writes an equally laudatory text a few days later when, '*Before coming back, I go to the top of the hill at Arromanches. It is such a beautiful sight that it makes me cry! The barrage balloons shine over me in a very blue sky, the great bridges of boats form jetties and quays in the sea.*' (June 22nd). Similarly, the Allied aviation spurred not only fear in her mind,

'*A cloud of English bombers goes over, filling the whole red sky. A very beautiful sight.*' (July 7th). Throughout the story, we are struck by the recklessness of its main character. As early as June 6th, she dares to cross the priory courtyard, then the street, under machine gunfire, to fetch tea to please a wounded English soldier. The same day, she tells of the French and British flags that she insists on raising despite the danger. Not forgetting her many comings and goings by bicycle on roads that are difficult to cross, except by military vehicles. And although she does not consider herself a heroine, she never gives the impression of being afraid, only expressing elation before extraordinary events, and varying feelings spurred by the host of characters (around 70) we meet throughout her story.

She has nothing but admiration for the British, constantly expressing the '*joy*' of being in their company. With these '*charming*' men (June 8th), '*the calm and smiling attitude of the English amazes me.*' (June 21st); she describes them as her '*friends*' (June 24th) with whom she spends nice evenings, greatly appreciating their temperament, '*The English are very kind to the workers, paying attention to the least complaint.*' (August 19th to 26th). Of course, her Anglophilia and her uncommon ability to speak with the liberators in their own language largely explain these excellent relationships. In fact, she notes that, '*the Canadians have great success in the village because they often speak French, but they are less distinguished than the English*' (June 12th, blue version). Between the latter and Marcelle Fauchier Delavigne, genuine affinity develops, '*I go to bathe in the river. Three Englishmen are there doing their washing; others, half-naked, are sunbathing. I chat with them for an hour.*' (August 11th). In other words, '*I cannot refuse them anything*' she writes as early as June 9th. They have a friendly relationship with one exception: when members of the Intelligence Service set up their kitchen in the chapel and chop meat on a tombstone, '*an underlying state of war*' is declared (episode mentioned in the blue version and in the first machine-typed version but not included in the published version, probably to avoid tarnishing the image of the British as a whole).

She is also very fond of the students at the garden Centre whom she often calls '*kids*' in preliminary versions (only once in the final version). On June 5th, '*a long, wearing day*', her heart stops when she discovers that '*poor little*' Gavet has been taken to the prison in Caen. Nevertheless, these young men also make their headmistress laugh, '*boots, spurs, gas masks, revolver holsters, lifebelts, have transformed our students into Martians.*' (June 7th). Whether she has to lecture them or be disturbed by the '*herd*' passing by (two occurrences), it clearly appears that, in these troubled times, her concerns are often turned to those whose well-being has been entrusted to her by their parents.

However, Marcelle Fauchier Delavigne is not so comfortable with her Norman neighbours. Could it be her Parisian origins or her wealthy extraction? On occasion, she is quick to pass harsh judgment on those around her or those who come from the outside. On June 23rd, even though the passage was not ultimately retained, she declares that the school's newcomers are '*ugly and pathetic. What a humiliation to be French.*' On the same day, on the subject of locals who refuse to lend their pianos, '*Nasty people [...]. Have the French always been like this?*' Elsewhere, she refers to a Norman family as '*mufles*'[3]. On June 7th, in a passage that was also later removed, she even goes so far as to give marks, out of 20, to several people around her. While the two students mentioned above score well above average, this is not the case of the adults... Overall, she seems very disappointed by the welcome given to the liberators by her compatriots, '*When will I find a truly enthusiastic French person who is not a too sensitive and judgmental person!*' (June 22nd, in the handwritten text – passage later deleted).

---

3. French saying, which can be translated as 'boors', used to describe bad-mannered people.

So, what can be said about Marcelle Fauchier Delavigne's feelings towards the Germans? She clearly has little animosity towards those she calls the '*Boches*'[4], as most French people at the time. Patriotic but not resentful, she offers a surprising description of one German lieutenant riding his bicycle past the priory. In her words, he is, '*a big green spider, cap and breeches tied up by wire!*' (black ink version, June 5th). She also writes these very moving lines when she comes across the corpse of a German soldier covered in dust. She is '*struck*' by '*his grey, closed face*', in the '*big sleep in action: no relation to a death in bed.*' (June 7th).

The two great absentees very dear to Marcelle Fauchier Delavigne's heart, who appear only in watermark in her diary, are also worthy of a few words. Over the years, the narrator has chosen to delete most of the references she initially made to her son, Jean, who fell in battle in 1940. No doubt out of modesty, she reduces these references from seven to two. Unfortunate perhaps, given the power of her prose in sentences like this one, not retained in the final version, '*It seems to me that Jean is present, that he took part in this liberation of France, which begins with this village he loved so much.*' (June 8th). Then, there is her husband, Emmanuel, whose nickname, Mano, is kept in her text. Here again, his presence is reduced to a minimum in the published version (a single mention – but what a mention – at the very end, on August 27th, the day of his return to Saint-Gabriel). In the first two versions, he is mentioned (openly or via references to his unoccupied room, where the British soldiers now sleep) 12 and 5 times respectively. However, the text needs to be reduced, and choices need to be made, the writer preferring to emphasise her outside activities to the detriment of family considerations.

Marcelle Fauchier Delavigne is a very active and mobile civilian who plays a significant role in organising the home

---

4. Name with a pejorative connotation given to the Germans by the French people during the First and Second World Wars.

front. Her mastery of English immediately offers her a special role. In Saint-Gabriel and the nearby villages, she is the obvious intermediary for the *'Tommies'*[5]. *'I meet an Englishman, two Englishmen, twenty Englishmen. I talk to them all, a new joy,'* she writes as early as June 7th. The next day, it is confirmed, *'They are glad to find someone who speaks English and ask me a lot of questions'* (June 8th). Then, while waiting to be given a precise assignment at the employment centre in Bayeux (late June – early July), she bicycles back and forth. *'I jump on my bicycle to act as an interpreter on right and left...'* (June 7th), gives news to the villagers who find shelter in a *'hole'* (June 7th), listens to the one and only radio in the Creully area (June 9th), is beware of rumours, preferring to wait for reliable information that does not always arrive, *'Since the Americans have been moving towards Paris, rumours spread out. Everyone shares sensational news, denied the next day... When I ask my Colonel about an advance, he always gives the same answer: "It may be..." Then, he smiles.'* (June 11th).

Although Marcelle Fauchier Delavigne is well informed thanks to her travels and numerous contacts, she focuses neither on military operations nor technical details on the liberating armies. The references to trench-digging work are removed from the final version and, apart from details on the regiment of the wounded soldier tended to on June 6th, she remains silent on the specific ranks and roles of the officers she rubs shoulders with throughout the period. By publishing her text, Marcelle Fauchier Delavigne strives to convey the memory of historic and troubled times, marked by encounters with a multitude of new people from very different backgrounds. Her account is also marked by the absence of those dearest to her: her husband, Emmanuel, her daughter, Colette, and her two grandchildren, Hervé and Alain, sons of the late Jean, who are only three and a half years old in the summer of 1944 and far

---

5. Slang for a common soldier in the British Army, used during the First and Second World Wars.

from Normandy, in Burgundy. Although little to nothing is said about these family members, it is undoubtedly for them that these notes are taken on a daily basis, then carefully reworked in the months following the end of the Battle of Normandy.

Julien Crué
From what Marcelle Fauchier Delavigne says in
Three months with the English –
On the occasion of the fiftieth anniversary of the D-Day
Landings, literary study of a testimonial, 1994,
by Anne-Marie Riss, professor, and holder of an *agrégation*[6].

---

6. The *agrégation* is the most competitive and prestigious examination for civil service in the French public education system.

INTRODUCTION

St. Gabriel is a small village with 200 inhabitants – less today for there are only elderly people, women and children. We live in a small and very green valley: just grass and apple trees. Nothing else. Across the river in front of us there is a fairly steep hill that leads to the next village. Then there is the plain, or rather a 3-kilometre long plateau, filled with large posts and mines, all the way to the sea: the deserted, the imprisoned sea enclosed by barbed wires that surround the beaches and these 'Mine' signposts with skull and crossbones.

You have seen the setting: now here are the characters. Old Normans, who fall to their knees when a plane flies low above their heads, think that the Vistula is a disease, and close their never-ending, unexpected and alarming forecasts with these enigmatic words, 'One might wonder...' The same little nest is home to three birds: the abandoned castle, the youthful and cheerful mill, and the garden Centre located in an old 16th-century priory[7] which is home to forty or so kids aged 12 to 17[8], M. and Mme Marze[9] and their son Bernard, – who educate and supervise them – and me[10], opposite the priory, in my small house, alone with my old Blanche[11], all waiting for the landings with as much faith as the first Christians waiting for a miracle.

And the miracle happened!

---

7. See back cover.
8. See pages 148-149.
9. Mme Marze is head of the garden Centre since its foundation in 1929. M. Marze, her husband, is a teacher there. See page 146.
10. See page 150.
11. See page 146.

Sunday, June 4th

Today there is a first communion at Saint-Gabriel. It is a fine day. All the children give the impression of having sore feet, they are no longer used to wearing shoes. Two mothers have come from Paris; they were machine-gunned on the way, and the train was ten hours late. They talk of nothing but bombardments and provisions. A leg of mutton evokes general joy and astonishment. It is as tough as old leather, but it is a leg of mutton! ... The Parisians marvel at it.

It is three o'clock, and I can't go on! I go off to Tracy[12] on my bicycle. A bomb has fallen beside the church, demolishing the old presbytery and leaving a huge crater.

A woman in her donkey cart and a little girl were killed while the donkey was unhurt...

> The machine-typed version provides two details that help set the scene.
> On one hand, the reference to the First Christian Communion hymn, one we would expect to hear on this occasion, *O salutaris Hostia,* hence its deletion from the final text.
> On the other hand, the context of the German occupation in Saint-Gabriel, that contrasts with the experience of the two mothers who have come from Paris for the occasion: the usual flight over the village by the British Air Force.

O salutaris Ostia[13]. *The children's voices are now accompanied by a steady rumble... 'It's the English...', we whisper. Any kid in the country can tell the difference between the noise of that friendly engine and the other one. But this visit has become so familiar that we no longer attach any great importance to it. (Machine-typed version.)*

---

12. Tracy is a village located on the Normandy coast, 2.5km from Arromanches. Suzanne de Bourgoing, born as Fauchier Magnan (Marcelle Fauchier Delavigne's sister-in-law) lives in the Fauchier Magnan's family property in Tracy.
13. The correct title is *O salutaris Hostia.*

When I get back I am told: 'Gavet[14] has knifed the Boche who supervises the students at forced labour.' What? ... Gavet? Poor little Gavet?... I question him. It seems that in a moment of irritation he threw down his spade; he had his pen-knife at hand to trim a finger-nail and it went with the spade. These are the facts. He tries to laugh to reassure himself but while he is speaking, the adjutant Spitz[15] and the sergeant come to find him to take him to headquarters at the château[16]. When we protest, Spitz adds: 'Don't go on about it, he must go, but he will certainly be back tomorrow morning, or perhaps this evening.'

What will become the Gavet episode has just begun.

While joking with Spitz, who has become quite familiar with everyone at the school, the Marzes insist that Gavé stay. (blue version).

In the blue-ink version, these two lines tell us about the relatively trouble-free cohabitation with one of the German officers, Spitz.
Mme Marze is the head of the horticultural school since its foundation in 1929. This school was established within the Saint-Gabriel Priory. M. Marze, her husband, is a teacher at the same school. They live on site. Jane Marze, whose name is recorded as 'Jeanne' on the 1936 census, studied in Nevers, successfully passing the 'Brevet supérieur'[17].

---

14. Gavet is a student at the garden Centre (see page 148).
15. Sergeant Major Spitz was probably a member of the German military staff.
16. The Château de Saint-Gabriel belongs to the family of the village mayor, M. Delacour, and is located on the edge of the village on the road to Bayeux.
17. The *Brevet supérieur* was, at the time, the French qualification to become a primary school teacher.

Monday, June 5th

Not only has Gavet not come back, but we hear that he is being taken to prison in Caen. As the lieutenant is cycling past the Centre. M. Marze asks him why Gavet has not been freed. 'He behaved in an incredible way. He turned up for his interrogation with both hands in his pockets: perhaps he's mad?' We try to persuade the officer that indeed he is not quite all there. A long, wearing day. I go to the workshop to continue the binding of my Nicholson dictionaries. This work seems to restore my mental equilibrium, and then, towards evening, I go back by the little 'snail road' (*le petit chemin des escargots*) to my dear fir wood[18]. It is dismal and cold.

'In the evening, following the "snail" path, I return to my dear evergreen grove.'

---

18. This evergreen wood can be found at the top of the hill near Villiers-le-Sec.

The handwritten version simply refers to the intervention that Yvanne, M. and Mme Marze's daughter, is about to attempt in Caen. By this point in time, everyone is optimistic that Gavet, whose name is spelled differently over time, including 'Gavé' in day-to-day notes, will soon return.

The machine-typed version reminds us that Marcelle Fauchier Delavigne is a woman of letters who can paint the portrait of a character in just a few words. Hence, the portrait of the easily imaginable lieutenant's silhouette!

'The lieutenant, a large green spider, with a cap and pants mounted on iron wire, cycling in front of the Priory.'

Meanwhile, in the handwritten version, Marcelle Fauchier Delavigne relaxes over some bookbinding, and sheds light on the extent of the German requisitions.

I continue my bookbinding (the Boches have taken my little stove), then I go for a walk along the Villiers coast (weather cold and cloudy). (Handwritten version)

The location of the little 'snail wood' is also indicated – along the coast, on the road leading to the neighbouring village of Villiers-le-Sec[19], located on the plateau.

---

19. Villers-le-Sec is located 2.8km from Saint-Gabriel, on the plateau by the sea.

Tuesday, June 6th

There is a huge glow from a fire behind the church[20]. It goes out quite soon, but gradually the noise gets louder, and becomes infernal. I don't know where to go. Everything is shaking and vibrating around me. It sounds as if the houses are going to collapse and I think several times that my last hour has come. but I am incapable of prayer. I curl up into a ball and that's all.

The poor little dog, Pat, is shivering beside me.

Around 3 a.m. a fire has started towards Frenay[21] and since 4 am unceasing and dreadful bombardments. (Handwritten version.)

At about six, as there is still a great racket, I decide it would be more sensible to go down to the kitchen[22], where I sit by the stove. It is starting to get light. Soon I see Madame Marze and Durot[23] coming in. 'Oh, Madame, it's the invasion,' says Madame Marze, very excitedly, 'come with us, quick.' We kiss. She hasn't been able to come over sooner because there was a German in front of the porch who wouldn't let anyone in. He has just left. I am still in my pyjamas, I get my clothes, my photo of Jean[24], and a book (Pascal's *Pensées*[25]), and get dressed in Madame Marze's bedroom. Then I find everyone in the refectory[26]. Great excitement. The students are all there and all talking at once. M. Marze can be heard shouting: 'Don't go near the windows.' … The noise is so deafening that it deadens that of the guns a bit. Madame Marze is full of excitement and can't keep still. I go with her to the porch for news. We find the Polish soldiers who live at the Centre and who tell us: 'It's the

---

20. See the village map page 143.
21. Fresnay-le-Crotteur, hamlet of Saint-Gabriel.
22. From her kitchen, Marcelle Fauchier Delavigne can see the priory's porch. It was closed every evening. See the priory's map page 144.
23. Durot, apprenticeship master at the garden Centre, worked the fields on the plains just outside the priory.
24. See photograph of her son, Jean, page 151.
25. This book, along all the other books mentioned in this account, are still in the library of her house of Saint-Gabriel.
26. See the priory's map page 144 and the photograph page 147.

invasion… the tommies will soon be here!' They are laughing a lot. They seem a bit drunk. And now the adjutant in battle dress, very pale, is about to go into the refectory… but someone calls him out and he has to go at once. I feel a chill seeing him go past. Ernestine and Madame Gravey[27] are frightened and would like to come to the priory. We go with Madame Marze to fetch them. The road seems different from usual; it is as if time had stopped still. In the Centre the kitchen[28] seems odd with all the village people in a corner, their little bags of treasures on their knees.

Marcelle Fauchier Delavigne takes with her a photograph of her son, Jean[29], Lieutenant of the Saumur cavalry school, *10e régiment de cuirassiers* (commanded by Colonel de Gaulle), killed in combat on May 20th 1940 in Parfondru, in the area around Laon (Aisne department). At that time of the D-Day, it is a way to associate him with the liberation of France.

The Adjutant comes and says goodbye to the children. He goes down to the kitchen in battledress, he seems very emotional. (Blue version.)

> This is probably the German officer who had good relations with the garden Centre and who played a part in the Gavet incident.

I go out again to ask after my faithful Blanche. At the corner of the Villiers-le-Sec road and in front of the café[30] I see some German soldiers with their helmets covered with leaves, slipping along hugging the walls. Blanche's house is shut up, with all the shutters closed.

---

27. Some of the village's inhabitants: Angéline Gravey lived on 25, rue de l'Église, her husband was a watchmaker. Ernestine Lecoutey was Blanche Lahaulle's sister-in-law, she was a linen maid and lived on 29, rue de l'Église.
28. See the map of the priory page 144.
29. A tombstone is located at the entrance of Parfondru, a small village in the Aisne department and 12km from Laon, where Jean Fauchier Delavigne was fatally injured. At the end of the war, his body was buried in the Saint-Gabriel cemetery.
30. See the village map page 143.

Dimanche 4 juin 1ère communion à St Gabriel. Je vais à Tracy
qui a reçu une bombe. Nous couchons.

lundi 5 juin — Gavé a été arrêté par les Allemands et em-
mené à Caen. Yvan va faire des démarches. Je continue
une reliure (les boches m'ont pris mon petit réchaud) et je
vais en procession sur la côte de Villiers (temps couvert
et froid) —

mardi 6 Vers minuit je suis réveillée par des bombardements assez lointains. Je me rendors un peu, vers 3h
lueurs d'incendie vers Fresnay, et à partir de 4h
terribles bombardements sans arrêt. Je finis
par descendre à la cuisine avec Pata. à 8h arrivent
Mr Marzy et Durot qui nous cherchent
et nous disent : c'est le débarquement ! !
Je suis encore en pyjama. J'emporte mes affaires
et les photos de Jean, et vais m'habiller dans
la chambre de Mme Marzy. Tout le monde est
rassemblé dans la cuisine, grande excitation.
Sa rentrée de Paris a allé au jardin. Des soldats
sont ivres et paraissent à l'arrivée des renforts méchants. Le lieutenant
est tué à Crépon dit-on. l'adjudant vient dire
au revoir aux enfants très émus. Nous voyons passer
des hommes qui se cachent le long des haies, des autos
des autres des Tanks allemands — peu peu

Page from Marcelle Fauchier Delavigne's diary, dated from June 6th.

"My faithful Blanche": Blanche Lahaulle belonged to one of the village's old families, she lived at 42 rue de l'Église. She acted as Saint-Gabriel's cook when Emmanuel and Marcelle Fauchier Delavigne were residing there. We will find her in front of her stoves on multiple occasions in the course of this account.

I go back quickly. I am a bit nervous. After seeing German motorcycles, cars, and tanks go past without stopping, nothing more; but towards Villiers we see tanks coming up and men hiding along the hedges. The firing gets louder. We are told it's at Crépon[31]. 'The lieutenant seems to have been killed.' It is midday, everyone sits down at the table but no one can eat. The battle is getting so close that we leave the refectory to go to the store-room entry[32], a little windowless room with walls a meter thick. We can follow the battle through a loophole. The firing goes on without a break. I think the windows are going to break. Suddenly one of the students tells me that the English have been seen on the hill. I look for them, but I can't make them out. A German tank is on fire[33].

At this point in the story, we must take into account the description that Marcelle Fauchier Delavigne makes of this day in the evening of the 6th of June in the pencil version.

We see men passing by and hiding along the hedges; motorcycles, cars, German tanks and little by little we see them passing by again the other way around. I search for Blanche, in vain. M. Felix[34] goes looking for some news. Gravet[35] and Augustin[36] ask to take refuge in the Centre, people say that the English are at Crépon. The guns hit harder and harder toward Villiers. I cannot eat anything at

---

31. Crépon: a village 5 km from Saint-Gabriel, on the plateau facing the sea.
32. See the map of the priory page 144.
33. See photographs of the coast of Villiers-le-Sec page 152.
34. Félix Féral, who lived at 2, rue de Creully. He was the father of Mme Marze.
35. This Gravet is probably Mme Gravey, who was mentioned before, as Marcelle Fauchier Delavigne didn't have a perfect knowledge of how all the villager's names were spelt.
36. There is no Augustin in the 1936 census of Saint-Gabriel, we don't know who this is.

The road to Saint-Gabriel

Organized in a combat group with the infantry of Colonel Meyer, a dozen self-propelled guns counter-attacked from Bayeux towards Ver-sur-Mer, going through Saint-Gabriel. On June 6th 1944, this unit is the only armoured reserve of the area. It is placed under the command of Colonel Meyer who leads the *915. Grenadier Regiment* (*352. Infanterie-Division*). They are stopped on top of the ridge above Saint-Gabriel in front of Villiers-le Sec, two assault guns are destroyed, numbers 222 and 223: they belong to 2nd Platoon, 2nd Battalion of tank destroyers of the German *352. Infanterie-Division* (numbering more than twenty self-propelled guns). This counter-attack would fail, they would go no farther than Bazenville. In the afternoon of June 6th, Colonel Meyer was killed. A Sherman tank, n° 44 of Lieutenant Charlton from B Squadron of the 4th/7th Royal Dragoon Guards, was destroyed in the combats on the heights to the north of the Seulles river. It was the Duplex Drive amphibious tank of Lieutenant C. Charlton, commanding the 1st Platoon, B Squadron of the 4th/7th Royal Dragoon Guards. It was destroyed by one of the two *Sturmgeschütz*, 222 or 223. In the fight, lieutenant Charlton and L/Cpl Day were wounded, and trooper Mathews was killed.

(These explanations were given by Jean-François Le Cuziat, President of the Ver-sur-Mer Museum.)

lunch. On the ridge, we can see German soldiers and tanks, the machine gun does so much noise that we leave the kitchen for the commissary entrance. I sit down in the office[37] where Durot and Berrier[38] come to see me on all 4. I can hear the windows shat-

---

37. Office, See the map of the priory page 144.
38. Berrier is a supervisor at the garden Centre.

tering. All of a sudden one of them tells me that we can see the English on the coast. I look but see nothing. (Handwritten version.)

A few minutes later, about five o'clock, I hear: 'There is an Englishman, there, by the kitchen wall. I go cautiously and see him through the little window on the stairs[39], behind the honeysuckle. My heart is beating so loud that I think he must hear it. I call out in English, he points his gun at me, then understands and signs to me not to come out, then others quickly appear, under the left porch[40], I rush towards them. They are all wet: 'I landed in the sea, for you', says one of them. I fly into his arms. They leave.

> It's around 5 pm when the first English soldiers enter the priory. "They swam across the Seulles": indeed, concerned that the bridge on the Seulles[41] could be trapped, they opted to swim across.

And then there are more and more, the garden is already full of them; among them, one is wounded slightly in the face; he seems exhausted and is shaking; we want to put him to bed in the kitchen, but he protests, he is afraid of making the bed dirty! We offer him whatever we have, but he only wants a cup of tea. Going to my house to get it, I cross the road amid the salvoes of machine-gunning. There is a blood-stain in front of the door. I run up the stairs… The stillness and silence of the invisible beings which fill my room today stun me. The 'Caroline Testouts[42]' are fading in the vase. When I get back I find the students crowded round the bed and translate the questions and answers. The wounded soldier wants to open his package of twenty-four hours' rations, to hand round: chocolate, sweets, biscuits, etc… Sadly, it is full of water.

> This paragraph alone sums up the behaviour of Marcelle Fauchier Delavigne: to bring some tea to a wounded English soldier, she doesn't hesitate despite the machine

---

39. See the map of the priory page 144.
40. See the vegetable porch on the priory map.
41. The Seulles river flows behind the pastures at the back of the priory and empties into the sea at Courseulles.
42. Name of a climbing rose bush species going up the side of her house.

gun salvoes, to leave the shelter of the priory, cross the courtyard, and rush into the street going to her house! This temerity, this recklessness, and this hospitality we will see all along this diary. In spite of all the risks taken, she takes the time to notice the pool of blood in front of her door… notably, in the definitive version we have a contemplation on silence and on the withering roses.

Having learned to speak English through her English nanny, she easily translates the exchanges between the wounded and the students.

At my suggestion English and French flags are put up at the office window. Suddenly there is an enormous explosion, a shell has just gone through the dormitory roof[43], and thick smoke is coming out. 'It's a fire, it's because of the flags,' cries Madame Marze. At the same moment a German appears at the door, he is distraught and asks if there are any English here; we all collect in front of the wounded man. A panicky student calls out: 'The Germans are back!' and there is a mass retreat to the staircase with our friend. The German has gone and the fire is out but I had a nasty fright! We lay the wounded soldier down again in the classroom. He is shivering all the time. He is soaked. I would like to get some alcohol from my house, but the machine-guns are sweeping the road. M. Félix has a little Calvados and gives it to him. We decide to get him out of his clothes but that means everyone except M. Marze has to leave the room. We come back to find him enveloped in an old jacket and trousers too big for him. While we dry his uniform in front of the stove he shows us his photos: views of Africa, where he went through the whole campaign in the Eighth Army. He comes from Yorkshire, and is in an elite regiment: 'The King's Own Yorkshire Light Infantry[44], and has two Ts on his sleeve, standing for two rivers, the Tyne and Tees[45]. He is worried and wants to talk to one of his mates from his regiment; I go to fetch one who is guarding the prisoners beside the canal wall. A German soldier is lying on

---

43. See priory map page 144 and photo page 147.
44. The exact name of this regiment is King's Own Yorkshire Light Infantry.
45. See page 154.

the ground, very pale, and seeming to be in pain. Near him I see the whole band of the old Poles happily sitting on the grass. It is apparently time for dinner, the wounded soldier sits down by me, I slaughter the beautiful British language, and this nice Englishman doesn't seem to mind. He drinks tea and is contented, and so am I! I should like to stop time at this beautiful moment. But now the Englishman wants to go back to his mates: his clothes are not yet dry, but never mind, he says he must get back to go on his way 'to Berlin.' Night has come. Everyone stands round him in the class-room[46] as he distributes English copper coins as mementoes. Then he leaves, but is soon back to spend the night with two of his mates at the Centre. A dozen of the villagers crowd into the store-room entry, a real gypsy encampment. I go to bed in the little infirmary[47] but neither I nor Pat get any sleep.

He is worried and wants to talk to another soldier from his regiment, I go fetch one who guards the prisoners along the canal wall, M. Marze is with me.

A wounded German is on the ground, very pale, he looks like he is suffering, near him I can see the group of old Polish soldiers, sitting on the ground and very cheerful. They get up to shake hands with Mme Marze. (Blue version.)

Meanwhile, the English made several prisoners, including the Polish soldiers who are more than happy to escape their forced service to the Germans, but they didn't lose their good manners as they get up to greet Mme Marze!
The night falls, some English soldiers, the wounded man among them, seek shelter in the priory, thus joining the villagers.

---

46. See priory map page 144.
47. See priory map page 144.

Liberation

The village of Saint-Gabriel was liberated by 5th Battalion The East Yorkshire Regiment, supported by B Squadron from 4th/7th RDG. According to the journal of the 5th Battalion, the village is entirely occupied at 5.50 pm on June 6th and many prisoners were captured, mainly from the German reconnaissance battalion and the *915. Grenadier Regiment* of the *352. Infanterie-Division.*

A short 20-second movie, shot by an AFPU (Army Film and Photographic Unit) cameraman on June the 6th 1944 as he was following the southward progress of the 69th Infantry Brigade, shows a column of "Tommies" from 5th Battalion The East Yorkshire Regiment entering the village and advancing along a wall. They are supported by Sherman tanks from B Squadron of 4th/7th Royal Dragoon Guards. After that, we can see the three buildings in front of the town hall. The Duplex Drive (amphibious) Sherman tank n° 40 of Major Jenkins, the B Squadron commander, cautiously advances and tries to turn into the street on the left. At this moment, there is an explosion in the street on the left of the tank, in front of the priory wall.

(These explanations were given by Jean-François Le Cuziat, President of the Ver-sur-Mer Museum.)

Wednesday, June 6th

6 o'clock. This morning the garden is full of tommies. Some are washing at the pump, some are gathered near the porch with their machine guns pointing at the gate. We are well protected. I learn that Blanche has found shelter with the Saints[48]. I go there. At the foot of the garden I see the entrance of a sort of burrow and at the

---

48. See map of the village page 143.

bottom of the burrow there is someone curled up. Blanche's voice calls out to me from far below. There are thirty-seven people in there! Some have just gone out for a bit of fresh air. They don't know about anything and are very glad to hear the news I bring them.

I search for Blanche. She has found shelter with the Saints family[49] *along with her granddaughters and the whole village. . I go down to the shelter door and I see little Oblet*[50] *curled up in the entrance, the whole village is here – 35 people. (Handwritten version.)*

It's the only shelter in the village. I go there. At the foot of the garden, I see the entrance of a sort of burrow, and at the bottom of the burrow there is the sacristan's wife, someone else, and a small and hunchbacked old lady curled up on herself. (Machine-typed version.)

> Both the pencil and machine-typed versions mention several persons being present with Blanche and her granddaughters, among the 37 (or 35) people hiding in the village's only shelter at the Saints' family home[51]: a young woman from the village and the sacristan's wife. All the others are in the priory dining hall.

Across the road, a corner of the Marie house[52] (*la maison Marie*) has collapsed. The road is full of German cartridges, grenades, rifles, thrown down, many of them broken, a complete picture of war.

However, almost all the houses are still standing, only a corner of the Marie house has collapsed. (Machine-typed version.)

> In the village centre, only one house was hit and just one corner was damaged.

I go to get two pitchers of water from the pump at the Centre and go to my house to wash. A peculiar silence in the empty house.

---

49. Some members of the Saint family lived at 27, rue de l'Église, and others lived route de Creully (Creully road) in front of the presbytery which is where the shelter was dug.
50. The correct spelling of her name is "Oblette", her mother is a teacher.
51. See village map page 143.
52. Marie Bouvet, 40, rue de l'Église.

I am struck by the way that everyday life has come to a stunned halt in the middle of this storm of fire. I am dying of hunger and open a can of sardines.

> The home of Marcelle Fauchier Delavigne usually bene-fited from a system of running water, linked to a pump. Because there was no electricity, she could only use the hand pump of the priory.

Going back to the Centre I find M. Marze exercising the magnificent horses that have been abandoned by the Germans, all saddled and wandering in the pastures. Poor M. Marze, he seems quite happy... Everyone is happy... The air we breathe is no longer the same.

I jump on my bicycle to act as interpreter on right and left... I meet an Englishman, two Englishmen, twenty Englishmen. I talk to them all, a new joy. At midday everyone hurries off to the Viel house[53], where the Germans lodged, and comes back with shoes, candles, socks, uniform jackets, torches, bags of barley, potatoes, equipment, bicycles, etc. There is a strange tribe moving round the paths at the Centre this evening: boots, spurs, gas-masks, revolver holsters, lifebelts have transformed our students into Martians.

There is a dead German on the road to Villiers, in front of the gate of the vegetable garden[54]. He is so covered in dust that I was going past without seeing him, and then his grey, closed face looking up at the edge of the road suddenly struck me. It is fine to start the big sleep in action: no relation to a death in bed.

> Marcelle Fauchier Delavigne is still a writer amid this turmoil, as it can be seen in her remark on the dead German and the beauty of this death in battle.

They say that there are still pockets of resistance at Bazenville[55] and at the château at Villiers.

---

53. Farm located near the priory which housed German soldiers.
54. See priory map page 144.
55. Bazenville, village on the plateau, 4 km away from Saint-Gabriel.

Marcelle Fauchier Delavigne on her bicycle. 'I jump on my bicycle to act as an interpreter right and left.'

Brother Germain[56] apparently wanted to kill X[57], Buon[58] was against it; X is the Germans' man, he has been seen going past with a basket towards the Grisard wood[59]. He was taking provisions to the Boches who are said to be hiding there.

I do some interpreting work for the Féral / burials / for Mme Roussel w[i]th a sick man, for Féral again to warn them of the presence of Ger[mans] in the Grisard grove. (Handwritten version.)

It seems that Marcelle Fauchier Delavigne is the only one in the village versed in the English language, this means that she acts as an interpreter for the English soldiers, but also for the village's personalities: Mme Féral, the mayor's

---

56. Brother Germain: unidentified character.
57. We have kept undisclosed the names of the villagers accused of collaborating in order to protect their families.
58. Buon: farmer for the Château de Saint-Gabriel on the far end of the village. *Cf.* Village map.
59. Bois Grisard, small grove near the entry to Saint-Gabriel from the Lantheuil village.

secretary, and Mme Roussel, the wife of one of the two owners of the village mill.

10 p.m. I finally get to my own bed, I can't go on any longer! It is wonderful weather. I have just seen a stream of tanks going past Marie Bouvet's house in a cloud of dust – a stream of deafening, stupefying, grinding metal. The road is turned into a ploughed field! Midnight… impossible to sleep. Planes… bombs … rockets… the thunder of anti-aircraft fire. I go to find M. and Mme Marze. They are in bed but think it is necessary to get the students up and take them to the store-room entry, the 'bombardment room'; as little Pépé calls it… The heat is unbearable. I grope my way to the linen-room[60], where I spend the rest of the night.

> In fact, Pépé (Claude Marze), their granddaughter aged only 3, called it "the bardment room", as Marcelle Fauchier Delavigne relates in the previous versions.

Gavet has just got back, on foot, from Caen. He only just avoided being shot. The Boches shot 150 prisoners. Gavet heard the names called and then the shots a few minutes after. At two o'clock in the morning they let out the rest of the prisoners. Caen is on fire. The Hotel d'Angleterre was one of the first buildings burnt. Gavet told us: 'I prayed all day along with the father of nine children. We were saved.'

> When Marcelle Fauchier Delavigne writes in her diary, the exact details on the massacre of the Caen prison's inmates, on June 7th, aren't completely clear, that is why she estimates that the figure of 150 victims Gavet gives her is correct. Later studies estimate the number of victims between 75 and 87 people.

A 65-year-old priest (abbot Victor Bousso), the Cnt of St Paul, etc. They wanted to take them too but they couldn't find any trucks. (Handwritten version.)

---

60. See priory map page 144.

Caen prison.

On June 6th, 1944, as early as 4 am, Captain Hoffman, then commander of the German part of the prison, is tasked with executing the orders provided in the case of maximum emergency. They state that the inmates under the jurisdiction of the *Gestapo* had to be evacuated by train to Germany as to not be freed by the Allies. The inmates awaiting trial before the court of the *Wehrmacht* were to be *"immediately released in case of an evacuation"* depending on the severity of the accusations, and the others were to be deported. As there are no trains or trucks left, four policemen of the *Gestapo* went there to shoot the prisoners under their service's jurisdiction. A list of around fifty people was drafted, likely by the doctor Harald Heyns, head of the Caen *Gestapo*. These executions took place in the small yards of the prison where they dug pits in the flower beds. The prisoners still in their cells could hear short machine gun bursts, followed by a pistol shot, while the next inmates were led by groups of six in the yard. The killing ceased around 10.30 a.m.

At 3 pm, "Albert", the *Hauptscharführer* von Bertholdi, brought with him another list from the *Kommandantur* and the massacre began again, emptying the cells until morning. During the night, 500 bombers of the RAF emptied their bomb bays on the city.

At last, at around 4:30 am, the prisoners whose file allowed it, among them Albert Gavet, were released by the captain Hoffmann. The others were evacuated to Paris, *via* Falaise.

At 5:45 am, the Germans had completely left the prison, but in the four yards, pits several meters wide were covered with quicklime.

We count a total of 76 victims!

(From *Massacres nazis en Normandie, les fusillés de la prison de Caen*, Jean Quellien and Jacques Vico (Charles Corlet, 1994).)

She mentions two names: a 65-year-old priest (the abbot Victor Bousso), and the count of Saint Paul (he must be Guy de Saint-Pol), both were executed by firing squad. Did Gavet know them, for their names appeared as soon as June 7th?

Nowadays this part is, alas, better known. Now, we know that Gavet had in fact very narrowly escaped death.

Thursday, June 8th

6 a.m. I go to my house with one of the boys who brings me a pitcher of water. My head aches. The noise is so loud that one cannot talk out of doors. From the window I see lorries full of German prisoners. The procession is unending, almost unimaginable. The vehicles are all different, from jeeps to great monsters bristling with guns, all marked with a white star.

My head aches from these 3 sleepless nights. (Handwritten version.)

Alone. I light the stove in the kitchen. Blanche is still hiding in her hole; I boil some water to make tea. (Blue version.)

> In the pencil version, then in the blue version, Marcelle Fauchier Delavigne elaborates on the state the last three days put her: her head aches! We can easily imagine it being the case as she writes: *"the noise is so loud that we cannot talk out of doors"*.

At 9 o'clock I go to the mill in hope of hearing the radio from London; it is the only place in the village that still has electricity. Bayeux was taken yesterday, without fighting. Back to the Centre: an Englishman is asking for potatoes, he is charming, I would like to give him all I have. The first note[61] of this new currency with a French flag on it has appeared and enchants me. Everything enchants me.

---

61. See page 158.

I would like to replace my two big flags at the priory but the Normans tell me: "The boches could have the bright idea to aim at the house, ..." so I placed the flags at my chamber's window, and every time an Englishman turns in the street, as soon as he spots this huge "Union Jack" he raises his head and smiles. (Machine-typed version.)

> This paragraph disappears in the final version, Marcelle Fauchier Delavigne will have other occasions to write about these flags and their emplacement. In her mind, they are the symbol of liberation and patriotism.

> Meanwhile:

The municipality is worrying because the dead are still not buried. I bike up to Creully, to ask the English on this matter. (Machine-typed version.)

At Creully, Etienne, the carpenter, who is marvellously well informed about the deeps and shallows along the coast, explains the prodigious system of this invasion. Coming back, I stop at the church in Saint-Gabriel. A shell has fallen in the choir and broken the statue of Saint Joseph. I see a wooden cross in the graveyard, marking the grave of an English soldier. Quickly home to get some flowers. Two soldiers come with me when I come back with some peonies. They are glad to find someone who speaks English and ask me a lot of questions, enquiring what I think of Pétain. How did the 'Jerries' (as they call the Germans) behave, and how is it that we don't seem to be starving? They give out quantities of chocolate, cigarettes, and sweets.

The kids run behind the jeeps, the soldiers get up and throw cigarettes and candies by the handful. A battle ensues behind the cars to pick up as much as possible. (Machine-typed version.)

During the course of the day, a walk into the country with Mme Marze, amidst gunfire and rumblings and roars of motors. We meet the Letulles[62]. Their farm is almost destroyed and all their

---

62. Letulle: their farm is also located in Fresnay-le-Crotteur's hamlet.

'On that sweet Fresnay road full of violets and mayflower bushes.'

animals killed. They are very well. No complaints. Mme Marze has seen two slightly suspicious cyclists. We warn the military police. There is a group of them at the Mairie corner. They ride motorcycles and wear very high, big helmets without any brims, quite different from the attractive flat tin hats that the other soldiers wear, which are covered with string all camouflaged with bits of brown and green cloth. From a distance they look like feathers.

At the side of the Fresnay road, three Englishmen have fallen and lie in the dust. Here at our home, on this pleasant and peaceful Fresnay road! Today it is white with dust, rutted, littered with guns, telegraph lines, with the posts knocked down, and unidentifiable murderous-looking and half- destroyed objects. An impression of disorder and ruin.

On this pleasant Fresnay road brimming with hawthorn and violets. (Machine-typed version.)

Poetry is never lost in her words.

I go with the English who want to visit the house of Mme X, and the Viel farm. They are looking for hidden Germans. At Viel the aftermath of plundering, horrible to see: there is only rubbish left, rotten meat in a bath-tub, and explosives: the English officer shows me the dangerous places. Night comes, and I go back through incessant thunders of noise to the Centre infirmary.

The Pézeril[63] family came to take a bedroom, their farm is in bad shape, so is Letulle's. I am going to sleep in the infirmary because the noise still hasn't stopped. Blanche goes back to her hole f[o]r the 3rd night in a row. (Handwritten version.)

> Contrary to the first impression that only one house was hit in the village, it now appears that the fights caused more damage, particularly on the two farms of the village. The villagers are disquieted, like Blanche who goes back to sleeping in her "burrow".

Friday, June 9th

A little sleep… I was so tired! A very loud bang woke me up at about midnight. I heard all the students going along the passage to the 'bombardment room', a loud noise as they pass, then the roll-call: 'Ladrette? present, Duval? present, Pierson[64]? present, etc. I go back to sleep.

10 am Ernestine shows me the damage on the church. A hole in the choir, two in the cemetery wall. (Handwritten version.)

> Every day, the combats continue and bring their share of damage: the church isn't spared!

In the morning I look for grenades in the road. They are everywhere. The English intend to recover their own and disable them, but they are not familiar with the German ones. The bomb-disposal teams will deal with them later. In the meantime I put beside each of them the little yellow flags with death's heads on them that the Boches have left behind. I feel myself to be a different

---

63. The Pézeril farm was also located in the hamlet of Fresnay-le-Crotteur.
64. They are some of the students present.

person. Everything seems to be changed. I speak to everyone. I love everyone.

Br[ea]kf[ast] with Blanche in the kitchen, during din[ner] Arrival of Phil[ippe] de B[ourgoing], everything is fine in Tracy. He has din[ner] with me. (Handwritten version.)

> Some days, Marcelle Fauchier Delavigne takes her notes very quickly, as is the case this Friday! Some common abbreviations followed by "Phil. De B." to name her nephew Philippe de Bourgoing!

At midday, while I am having lunch at the kitchen table with Blanche, someone comes to look for me to deal with three Englishmen. They are asking for white bread and chicken! Not very convenient. But I cannot refuse them anything. I tell Blanche to make the bread and manage the impossibility of finding a chicken.

I cannot refuse them anything. I tell Blanche to bake them some bread with all the flour she has left, and to only come back before me when she will have found a chicken. (Machine-typed version.)

> Here we can read that Marcelle Fauchier Delavigne can also give orders! In the definitive version, she moderated her language… *"only come back before me"* becomes *"manage the impossibility"*!

At 4 o'clock, I go up to Creully in a fog of dust and a torrent of trucks. I find Fauvart, Rambert, Marchal, Jamin, the good, the pure, and I talk… I talk…. I think I have never talked so much. General Montgomery goes past along the road in his black beret, I want to kiss him… Then it is in a little lean-to of the Paillaud[65] dairy, with broken windows, that I hear the news together with all the inhabitants of Creully: the Allies are at Formigny.

> As early as the 8th of June, General Montgomery, head of the 21st Army Group, established his headquarter in the park of the Creullet castle, directly in front of the Creully

---

65. The Paillaud dairy farm produces, since 1912, cheese and sterilized milk stored in cans.

Formigny

Located 5km to the south of Omaha Beach where the American troops land on June 6th, the village of Formigny is liberated three days later on June 9th. To achieve this, no less than three battalions worth of infantry and Sherman tanks were necessary to beat the German defences.

castle. From there, he oversees all the operations of the battle of Normandy.

Formigny is taken, some parts of Caen still resist. People say that Bayeux is covered with flags. I must make some f[o]r St Gabriel. 7 o'clock. They bury three Englishmen along the Fresnay road. The Roussel are floundering and lay flowers. Mme Roussel is always talking about them. I go for dinner at Bernard's[66] with the English medic. (Handwritten version.)

I listen to the London radio together with all the other inhabitants of Creully! The London radio! ... These beloved messages which were banned in France but where nonetheless listened to all over the country! ... Today they announce that the Allies have taken Formigny. (Machine-typed version.)

I learn that we can listen to the radio at 5:30 in the Paillaud factory where they have electricity.

While waiting for this, I help to make three flags which are going to be placed in the hand of the poilu at the war memorial. (Blue version.)

The definitive version lacks her words on the "beloved" messages from Radio London and the making of the three flags. American, British, Canadian? They are to be

---

66. Bernard Marze, son of the garden Centre's owners, also teaches there.

compared with the flags put atop the tower of justice of the priory: American, British and ... Russian[67].

Going back I find that the English soldiers at the side of the Fresnay road are being buried. I go there, I thought it would be worse... so beautiful, so simple, so great, this burial without undertakers. Man and the earth: that's all. What need of more? A pastor says prayers and everyone brings flowers.

Back home, I learn that English soldiers are being buried in the grass along the Fresnay road. I go there. A scene which reaches the epitome of greatness by its very simplicity. So beautiful, so pure, so grand is this burial with no undertakers. Man and earth: that's all. Why do more? Two soldiers wrap their comrade in his coat and lay him down. A pastor says a prayer, and everyone brings some flowers. (Machine-typed version.)

The typed version has more details, including details on the gestures the soldiers have for their dead brother in arms. We cannot forget in this moment that Marcelle Fauchier Delavigne lost her son Jean around Laon, on the 20th of May 1940, where he was buried. Maybe that she sees in this scene the ceremony that was possibly made for her son?

Very noisy and disturbed night. During the short intervals of silence I hear the clear little call of the toads. Three times the students troop past to the shelter. The house shakes.

The night is still as noisy and turbulent, but the toads bring out the big guns, between two detonations I can hear their strong voice. Then, three times the students troop past to the

'In the rare moments of silence, toad calls can be heard.'

---

67. See page 154.

shelter. AA fire is intense. The house shakes and once again the toad sings. (Machine-typed version.)

> On this evening, she pays attention to all the sounds coming from the night: the detonation of AA shells, the noise of the passing herd of students and the soft song of the toad!

Saturday, June 10th

Mme Roussel tells me that the 1st Englishmen are entering the priory. Heavy fighting in and around Caen, progress in Manche and beyond Bayeux. … Mme Féral makes an inventory of what was taken at Viel's today.

She says that there is a representative of de Gaulle at Creully with 2 Englishmen. Yesterday, I met there two French from de Gaulle's army. (Handwritten version.)

> It is strange to discover the date given by Mme Roussel for the English settling inside the priory. Where was Marcelle Fauchier Delavigne then? Did the English troops settle in the priory without her approval? This is very strange… This information will never reappear after that.

> Here we learn some news from the combats happening the same day in both Caen and Bayeux, as well as the presence of French troops in Creully as soon as June 10th. However, General de Gaulle will only come back on French soil on June 14th.

I go to the mill to have some news… I go back home and find Gavé with a wounded shoulder; a bullet went through it as he was talking with an Englishman while looking at the machine gun. (Handwritten version.)

Another episode on Gavet! Once again, his clumsiness is to blame. After the knife, a machine gun turned against him!

Morning. I have just seen the most beautiful sight in the world: under a threatening sky and hundreds of silver barrage balloons[68] (*saucisses d'argent*) the whole English fleet covers the sea as far as the eye can see. I made the journey to Ver-sur-Mer[69] by bicycle, slipping between the strings of boats on wheels, tanks, cars, going over piles of earth thrown up by these enormous caterpillars that push a gigantic horizontal plough in front of them, immediately opening up new roads. At the top of the hill in Ver, I thought I was dreaming when I found myself confronted by this marvel that men have been able to conceive and carry out. Between all the big ships move more thousands of amphibious vehicles that on water look like boats but once on shore begin to go on wheels; other boats open at the front and spew out unnamed equipment. On both sides of the road the slopes are covered with tents, various machines, odd-shaped apparatus. Men perched on a wall are sending morse signals. It could be a gigantic swarming antheap. Going back we meet infantry marching in single file along the road.

> In this long description of the bustling beach as seen from the coast of Ver-sur-Mer, Marcelle Fauchier Delavigne removed from the definitive version a geographical precision that she isn't entirely sure of: from Arromanches to Courseulles[70] and…? She also removes a precision on the name of the boats on wheels: the "ducks". Nonetheless, her descriptions allow us to easily imagine what these scenes, that we can watch nowadays on archive footages, looked like in reality.

---

68. They are airborne barrage balloons inflated with gas and linked to steel cable: they help prevent low-flying attacks by enemy planes. They could be charged with explosives. See page 153.
69. Ver-sur-Mer, village 10 km away from Saint-Gabriel between Asnelles and Courseulles.
70. Courseulles, a coastal village 12 km away from Saint-Gabriel.

4 p.m. I have just seen the most beautiful sight in the world: under a threatening sky and hundreds of silver balloons the whole English fleet covers the sea from Arromanches all the way to Courseulles and beyond. (Handwritten version.)

I made the journey to Ver by bicycle with Mme Roussel and 3 young girls. We slip between the "ducks", a sort of boat on wheel, tanks, cars… (Blue version.)

When I get back, 3 Englishmen are happy to hear me speak. F[o]r them, I go and search for some eggs. (Handwritten version.)

> Clearly, issues of language and food are significant for the soldiers on French soil. We can understand that they grew tired of their rations[71] and that they prefer our eggs, cheeses and chickens…

Tonight, despite the planes and guns, I slept, worn out. Suddenly, at 5, a brutal awakening. Five bombs have fallen in Saint-Gabriel; two in the pasture by the canal just behind the Centre[72]. A terrifying crash. Clatter of broken glass. We all hurry to the store-room entry. No harm done.

Tonight, despite the planes and guns, I slept a little in the Centre's infirmary, but suddenly, at 5, I'm brutally awakened. Five bombs have fallen in St Gabriel; two in the pasture by the canal just behind the Centre […] (Blue version.)

And behind the Colet's house.[73] (Handwritten version.)

> Once again, Marcelle Fauchier Delavigne sleeps in the infirmary where she feels less lonely, as night fighting continues above her head.

---

71. See page 157.
72. See priory map page 144.
73. Colet's house: we are not aware of its exact location.

Sunday, June 11th

This day completely vanished from the definitive version. However, this day is important to know the state of mind of both the villagers and the soldiers at Saint-Gabriel and Creully.

This morning, Blanche is distraught and upset as she counts her broken windows. . She thinks that her house is targeted, right in the bombs' trajectory! Of course, she was not there tonight but at the bottom of her shelter.

At mass, music is organized by Mlle Roussel. Te Deum, *and after mass, "la Marseillaise" … And no "God save the King". Some English soldiers, a lot of people gathering around them.*

I go to the pasture by the Canal to see the sinkhole made by the bombs. Not very big. Englishmen coming to visit the whole day. Widespread joy when a French-speaking Canadian arrives. He doesn't have any English accent but a heavy accent not unlike Auvergnat.

8:30 pm blessings at church, then a speech. Marseillaise. "God save the King" *in front of the War memorial. The square is covered with soldiers. I sit down with them while we wait for church to end, and they ask me questions about the state of mind of the French? On the German's behaviour? I can feel that they are not sure about the Normans. It seems that their welcome was quite cold. Some women shot at English soldiers as they landed! But they are all so charming! In the street, I saw a poster of the beautiful Order of the Day from General Eisenhower. (Blue version.)*

While bicycling home, I encounter on the chemin de Marie Chalot[74] villagers carrying mattresses, duvets, pillows. They are going to spend the night in the trench-shelters the Germans made. (Machine-typed version.)

---

74. Road to Marie-Charlot: the house of Marie Charlot is located rue du Bout-Cachard (or Bourg-Achard, the exact spelling is unknown). The location of the road itself is unknown.

Supreme Headquarters Allied Expeditionary Force

Soldiers, Sailors, and Airmen of the Allied Expeditionary Force!

You are about to embark upon the Great Crusade, toward which we have striven these many months. The eyes of the world are upon you. . The hopes and prayers of liberty-loving people everywhere march with you. In company with our brave Allies and brothers-in-arms on other Fronts, you will bring about the destruction of the German war machine, the elimination of Nazi tyranny over the oppressed peoples of Europe, and security for ourselves in a free world.

But this is the year 1944! Much has happened since the Nazi triumphs of 1940-41. The United Nations have inflicted upon the Germans great defeats, in open battle, man-to-man. Our air offensive has seriously reduced their strength in the air and their capacity to wage war on the ground.

Your task will not be an easy one. Your enemy is well trained, well equipped and battle-hardened. He will fight savagely.

Our Home Fronts have given us an overwhelming superiority in weapons and munitions of war, and placed at our disposal great reserves of trained fighting men. The tide has turned! The free men of the world are marching together to Victory!

I have full confidence in your courage, devotion to duty and skill in battle. We will accept nothing less than full Victory!

Good luck! And let us beseech the blessing of Almighty God upon this great and noble undertaking.

(General Dwight D. Eisenhower, order issued the day before D-Day to the Allied soldiers taking part in the invasion.)

I will not rest yet today! Superb weather. A lot of new arrivals today. ((Handwritten version.)

> As she recounts her day, Marcelle Fauchier Delavigne writes about the English settling little by little, as it was announced by Mme Roussel the day before.

Is this really the road in Saint-Gabriel? A swarm of berets!… When the traffic block in front of the porch has cleared, a lorry comes in carrying a bridge, a tank, and some other vehicle, one can see nothing but berets. … All the troops wear them: black for those in tanks, dark red for the paras, and khaki for all the others. The Scots have a pompom. Only the RAF in grey-blue wear a forage cap or peaked cap. And in every pasture one finds them camping along the hedges. They put up tents beside their lorries and live there with a little stove to cook on, tinned food etc. In the morning they do physical training on the grass and go to bathe in the river. One meets them all along the roads, continually repairing the damage that is done again next day. They are friendly, simple, placid, and cheerful.

A lorry carrying a bridge (together, they were taller than our house). (Machine-typed version.)

> The observation on the size of the bridge is quite impressive!

Today a nice RASC captain[75] (Captain Hemming) comes to ask me for accommodation. I offer him all I have – the big projection room and the new dormitory[76] at the Centre and all the free rooms in our house.

> Hospitality is the rule with Marcelle Fauchier Delavigne. At the Centre, she makes the rooms that are not used by the students available, and:

---

75. RASC: Royal Army Service Corps.
76. See priory map page 144.

In our house the 4 bedrooms as well, seeing as I'm alone here. (Machine-typed version.)

A chaplain and an officer reside at Mano's house and the Major at Jean's. They are all reserved and charming. (Handwritten version.)

Numerous lorries arrive during the day. They are hidden under all the priory apple-trees and in the yard. There is a continuous racket. Getting the rooms ready with Blanche, we discover that during the fighting a German broke the lock of the little ground-floor room and fired a bullet through the door.

He must have been wounded because there are still some bloodstains. (Machine-typed version.)

> For a long time, the door to the little ground-floor room kept the mark of the bullet hole!

Here are two more Englishmen; they are resting for a moment in the room and when I am called out I offer them English books and the first *Daily Mail* that M. Marze has just given me. The captain has lunch with me and shows me the photographs of his wife and little boy.

He has a thin moustache and smiling eyes. (Machine-typed version.)

In the evening Major Chapman arrives: the padre[77] with gold-rimmed glasses, very soft voice, and silent walk, and Captain Oeking, young, bronzed, cheerful, and [in English] 'good-looking'... They are very interested in tales of German behaviour, our life during the occupation, and our impressions of the day of the invasion.

> Once more, the descriptions are so accurate that we could draw Captain Hemming, the father, and even Captain Oeking[78].

They are all reserved and charming. All around us there is an incredible and labouring hive. Lorries all around the Centre.

---

77. Padre: priest who accompanies the soldiers.
78. Oeking, also spelt Ocking.

Cannons, bombs and planes are incessantly harassing us, it is a bit frightening. (Handwritten version.)

If Mano could see me preside over this table full of Englishmen at dinner, he would be so happy! Why isn't he here! (Blue version.)

It's one of the few moments where Marcelle Fauchier Delavigne voices her feelings. Notably the absence of her husband, Emmanuel, nicknamed "Mano", who is kept in Paris for professional business. Maybe there is a bit of the English reserve here, learned from her governess?

In the evening, for the first time in six months, since the Germans stopped our post, we can, despite the absence of electricity, hear the news thanks to the English. The Americans are advancing towards Cherbourg. Hard fighting near Caen. A very noisy and almost sleepless night.

The English place a device in front of Bernard's[79] door and plug it on a car battery. (Blue version.)

The radio plugged onto the battery.

---

79. See priory map on page 144.

Thus, sitting in front of the porch arch, everyone, French and English, can hear the news.

Where are our poor radios, the ones we handed over after breaking them, all of them: Father Félix took his to the town hall, attached to a string. He dragged it behind him, like a stubborn dog. (Machine-typed version.)

Another very noisy and almost sleepless night. The students get up three times. I spend the night at the centre, like every other day. Impossible to sleep. German bombings (Handwritten version.)

> Marcelle Fauchier Delavigne prefers to sleep near the students, as she has become accustomed, while the nightly battles continue, leaving the English comfortably accommodated in her house!

Tuesday, June 13th

Overcast in the morning, better in the evening. Very strong west wind.

… which usually unleashes the storm, but nothing alters the perfectly good mood of my companions. (Machine-typed version.)

My officers and the chaplain seem to appreciate Blanche's cooking, asparagus, strawberries and cream, and Calvados in particular.

> We can understand the good mood of the British officers, considering the dishes served to them… The strawberries probably grown in their hostess's garden, in front of her house. Strawberry plants could still be found there in the 1970s.

Blanche, flattered to cook for the English officers and to mend their pajamas, is somewhat reassured, although she still falls to her knees when a low-flying plane passes over her head as she is picking a salad. (Machine-typed version.)

She sleeps every night in a shelter. (Handwritten version.)

Churchill in Normandy

The British Prime Minister had wished to go to Normandy with the troops on June 6th. Only King George VI managed to dissuade him by stating that, if Churchill landed that day, he would go too! The "Old Lion" eventually admitted that it was not a good idea.

His first visit took place on June 12th: the head of state made an initial tour of liberated sites and visited Montgomery's headquarters at the Château de Creullet in Creully, very close to Saint-Gabriel. Churchill returned to Normandy on July 22nd and 23rd, passing through Caen, Cherbourg, Arromanches and therefore, Saint-Gabriel.

This evening on the news we hear an account of American exploits at the landing. Near Colleville[80] they were held down on the beach for 24 hours. Guns are firing all the time near us, although the Americans are at Carentan and the British at Balleroy and on the edge of Caen. Mr Churchill is in Normandy. While we are listening, a plane crashes in flames in the pasture by the canal. Tonight I sleep a little despite the noise, I am so tired.

After dinner, the English radio set is brought outside, in front of Bernard's house. (Handwritten version.)

Wednesday, June 14th

Beautiful weather. The night was almost calm. At 9:30am, I go to Creully to fetch groceries. The English traffic is so dense that it's hard to make your way along the road. The weather is turning. It's quite cold. (Handwritten version.)

---

80. Colleville-sur-Mer, the Omaha Beach, is 32 km from Saint-Gabriel.

A lot of wind all the time. Our staff has just been completed by a new, plump, and very cheery captain, Captain Grose[81]. We put a third bed in one of the bedrooms. These officers make many apologies for sharing my food, they are waiting for the arrival of their colonel to organise their mess and their cooking out of doors, which is the rule in their army.

Arrival of an additional captain. (Third bed in Mano's room). They are very nice, very cheerful at the table, and appreciate Blanche's cooking a lot. Since she has been kept busy, she is feeling much better. (Handwritten version.)

> Once again, we note the great attention Marcelle Fauchier Delavigne pays to the people around her.
> She also provides information on the officers' organization, as they wait for their colonel to arrive, to establish more durable living conditions!

The battle is still very fierce round Caen. The news this evening at a quarter past nine tells of some slight losses of ground. I learn from the English priest that General de Gaulle was in Bayeux today. The night is very tough, without a break; German aircraft buzzing around, salvoes of anti-aircraft fire followed by the noise of the students going past, the noise of bombs near or far, a few moments of quiet, then it all starts again. During the short periods of silence, the song of the toads.

[…] I cannot stay with the students in the 'boarding room' where about fifteen people are already sleeping because the smell is unbearable. I sleep in the infirmary with Pat, who is completely disoriented. (Machine-typed version.)

---

81. This captain's name is also written Gross.

Thursday, June 15th

The sun rises against a red sky. How good it is! I go to the 6 o'clock mass said by the Benedictine padre. We knock at the door of father Toncret, the old bell-ringer, to get the key of the church from him. The church is entirely empty. From the door I am struck by its gentle warmth. Nothing is changed, it still smells of dust and dry wood, and yet everything is different... They are here!

> For Marcelle Fauchier Delavigne, her day is limited to this beautiful day. She does not seem to find it useful to share her feelings or her actions. The rest we owe to the previous versions.

Alone in the church with Jean, who feels so close to me. I receive Communion, such great sweetness. (Handwritten version.)

> The memory of her son, Jean, who died in battle for France, was likely to come to her mind over these days when the battles continue.

Mme Level arrives from Audrieu[82], where fierce combat is being waged[83]. She comes to ask me for vegetables and settles at the Château. (Machine-typed version.)

> Mme Level lived at the Château d'Audrieu, which was requisitioned by the Germans to accommodate an SS re-connaissance unit. Her husband, Philippe Livry-Level[84] (1898-1960), a Resistance fighter, is then a pilot for Free France. To shelter her children from the fighting, she goes to the Château of Saint-Gabriel[85], where one of her daughters, Solange, the wife of Robert Delacour, lives.

---

82. Audrieu: a village located 9 km south of Saint-Gabriel.
83. The fighting in the area around the Château d'Audrieu was followed by the execution of nearly 90 British and Canadian prisoners until June 10th.
84. The name 'Livry' added to his name Level is that of a village in Calvados and one of the nicknames given to him in the Resistance, which he joined in 1940.
85. We found it quite pleasant to live in a place that the war had spared. The furniture was intact, the dishes were in good condition, and there were clothes. [...] Life went on, the vegetable garden was filled with vegetables, the cherry tree was laden with fruit, the strawberries were ripe, and the farmers, unsure of how to sell their fruits, were only too willing to supply us' Excerpt translated from a book by Monique Corblet of Fallerans (born Livry-Lebel), Voyage nocturne au bout du parc: d'Audrieu à Ravensbrück, Heimdal, 1994.

I go to Bayeux to gather the Normandy people's impressions on General de Gaulle. The road is impassable, ploughed-up on the edges, and constantly occupied by two lines of trucks going in opposite directions. I spend 25 minutes pressed against a wall at the entrance to the town, while the convoys parade by… the people of Bayeux don't seem very enthusiastic. They find de Gaulle haughty, dry, and cold, and prefer General Koenig. Tommies crowd the streets of Bayeux. (Machine-typed version.)

At the time of publication, Marcelle Fauchier Delavigne gives up on the idea of mentioning the people of Bayeux's opinion of General de Gaulle. We do not know the exact date the book was released by the *Renaissance du Bessin* presses: 1945, 1946? At the time, General de Gaulle was presiding over the Provisional Government of the French Republic (3rd June 1944 - 27th October 1946), and any such comment probably seemed inappropriate.

Now there is a genuine gathering in front of Bernard's door at the time of the radio broadcast. All the locals are there. After listening to the news, I go back for tea with the English. A very noisy night, but I spend it at home. (Machine-typed version.)

Why this return home? Is it related to the 'unbearable smell' mentioned the day before, and which made her abandon the 'boarding room' for the infirmary?

Friday, June 16th

This morning, I go up to Creully for supplies. On the way, I meet a Scottish infantry regiment marching along the edge of the road. They go in single file with the bagpipe at the head; the piper wears a little pleated skirt (*la petite jupe plissée*: i.e. a kilt). Sweet music, fragrant of heaths and heather. In the town I have difficulty getting around among all the convoys. At every crossing, Englishmen with big white sleeves and red helmets act as traffic police. The weather isn't good, a lot of wind from the west, a bit of rain. During the day the officers get their mess ready, I bring them flowers. One of them tells me that he has just met the king of England with General Montgomery on the Tierceville[86] road.

> Major pages in history reappear in Marcelle Fauchier Delavigne's notes. After General de Gaulle's visit to Bayeux on June 14th, she tells the story of King, George VI's, who came to Creullet to meet Montgomery in his headquarters[87] and the British troops.

At 5 o'clock, the arrival of a very big and jovial new major, Major Hodgson.

How many of us will be dining together tonight? I don't know. Blanche outdoes herself. (Blue version.)

I give out round the village several flags I have had made. We wait for the colonel until 9. The radio is brought into the room where we have dinner and the whole village gathers in the garden to hear the news through the open window.

Finally, wanting to sit down and not miss the famous 'This is London...' We bring a truck into our yard, the whole village listens to the news in front of our open window. (Machine-typed version.)

> And the importance of listening to the news with the entire village persists. Thus, the typed version specifies that, on that evening, the village no longer gathers in the courtyard of the centre to listen to the news, but rather in the courtyard of Marcelle's house, in front of the priory.

At 10 the colonel arrives with a young doctor and Captain West. The colonel says little, has a big moustache and takes snuff. Three more officers needing accommodation!... And the house is already full!...

---

86. Tierceville: a village on the outskirt of Creully on the road to Courseulles.
87. Montgomery's headquarters, where, on June 12th, he welcomed, the British Prime Minister Winston Churchill, then General de Gaulle on June 14th, General Eisenhower on June 15th, and finally, King George VI.

Four sleep in Mano's room. Two in the small bedrooms. One in the hall. The night is relatively calm. I spend it in my bedroom. (Handwritten version.)

There is great concern about material this Friday: supplying provisions for the guests and organising the house to meet accommodation needs. We learn a few names along the way, but their regimental affiliations remain unknown.

Saturday, June 17th

Eight English officers are staying here: the colonel, two majors, two captains, one priest, and a doctor. I have lunch with them again in the hall, but it's prepared by their own cook. Blanche is frantic. Tonight, they will dine under the tent in the priory. Some rest over the day. I go to deliver a flag to Marie Bouvais[88]. (Handwritten version.)

Today the arrest of X and his daughter is reported. Great excitement.

On the corner of the street, women in groups watch the gendarmes pass by… Some shout… 'Down with the Boches, down with X…'. (Machine-typed version.)

Visit from an officer stationed at Creully who wants to find out about the attitude of the French. He questions me a lot. He is shrewd and agreeable. This is what the lady at one château said to him: 'I hope you won't do any more damage than the Germans. They were very correct.'

Then, 'I'm waiting for the moment when reconciled with the Germans, you will go to war against the Russians' … He asks me if I think the French are happy about their arrival!… Alas!… He has doubts … (Machine-typed version.)

---

88. This could refer to Marie Bouvet.

I try to make a joke of this idiot, who is unworthy of being French. We laugh together.

> We learn from the arrest of collaborators and statements by a chatelaine that, during the German occupation, certain inhabitants taking sides with the occupiers.

Now our headquarters has set up the officers' mess in a tent in the priory yard, the cook has built a little oven out of doors, at the corner of the porch, and that is their kitchen. Beautiful evening. A crowd in front of the low wall to listen to the news. Progress in the Channel. From my bed I can still hear the bagpipe, he plays one, then another tune … sad, nostalgic… and now the anti-aircraft fire begins again.

A rather ordinary evening!

Sunday, June 18th

The church is full of very reverent English. The padre looks after them.

They march, carrying their berets beneath their shoulder patches. (Machine-typed version.)

The arrival of 500 refugees is announced. Everyone is summoned to clean up the Viel farm. Weather overcast and cold.

The well-meaning ladies busy themselves, aprons around their waists and brooms in hand, setting an example. (Machine-typed version.)

> The question of the refugees who escaped the bombings in the city of Caen is mentioned for the first time. The figure of 500 seems huge for a village that has not more than 300 inhabitants at the time…

I sense a certain preoccupation among the officers. A few words that slip from one of them cause me some anxiety. He is thinking about the possibility of defending the Centre. Yet the news from the Manche aera is excellent. The Americans have got to the coast near Carteret and cut off Cherbourg, but around Caen the Germans are hanging on furiously. They are sending their new invention against England: a pilotless plane which is causing damage there.

Tonight, while I listen to the English news with the English people, in front of Bernard's house at 9 p.m., the colonel wants to take me to their tent to drink some liqueur with him. He is charming, affable, and so well-mannered. He tells me that upon his arrival, he loved, entering the hall and seeing all the officers around the table where I was sitting. It seems to me that the welcome extended by the Normans in general, must have been quite cold. They are terrified and wonder if the Germans were not paying more. Heavy gun fire during the night and a visit from Boche planes. I go from my bed to the sofa several times, then I fall asleep. (Handwritten version.)

Once again, in the final version of this paragraph, originally written in pencil, the judgment on the behaviour of the local inhabitants is erased.

While I am listening to the radio in the evening, the colonel comes to find me and take me to the mess in the tent. Extremely friendly and polite, as they all are, he tells me how pleased he was to get here and to see all his officers around me at the table. Again a terrible night, little sleep.

Monday, June 19th

Marcelle Fauchier Delavigne makes no mention of this day in the final version. However, in her journal, she had written what follows:

This morning, it's raining, very bad weather all day despite very strong easterly wind. I rest and read Stendhal by Alain. It's difficult to find a reading that can engage my mind. During lunch, Major H... comes to keep me company. He is charming, speaks softly, his refinement offers true relief. The little captain with the thin moustache then comes to ask if I could accommodate two more officers.

Together, we empty the small room under the vault. It's a bit like a game. He is cheerful, we have fun, feel alive again. At 6 p.m., they rush to tell me that Bobomme[89] has fallen into boiling water. I immediately bring the English doctor. Fortunately, nothing serious, the doctor and the kind captain are attentive. Excellent supplies spur the admiration of all the Marze.

Good news tonight, the Americans are 12 kilometres from Cherbourg, still fiercely fighting between Tilly and Caen. Champenois de Villers[90] heard that Caen was entirely occupied by the English, but that Germans were still hiding in houses and shooting from the windows. (Handwritten version.)

Every evening, many soldiers come to visit, chatting. I hand out some butter, eggs, cheese [two lines crossed out]. They eventually tire of their canned food, which is excellent by the way, and their biscuits. In exchange, they give me chocolate, cigarettes, soap! What a joy to have real soap! I have never felt in such completely in harmony with everyone. (Blue version.)

Many dead in the streets and Caen on fire. Fairly calm night. Wind. At 3:30 a.m., heavy gun fire and planes overhead. I go to the sofa and fall asleep again. (Handwritten version.)

Tuesday, June 20th

Just like the previous day, this one is not included in the final version.

It is true that the notes taken that evening seem more disjointed, as if moral fatigue was setting in after fifteen days without real progress from the Allies, and an 'ordinary' life is emerging, to the point that photography is the only activity that seems to have meaning to immortalize the present! We can understand why Marcelle Fauchier Delavigne preferred to remember nothing of this 'ordinary' day...

---

89. Bobomme: one of the priory students.
90. Champenois de Villers: more likely Paul Champonnois, from Villiers-le-Sec.

It's been fifteen days since they arrived! The weather is quite cloudy, but it's not raining. Strong wind. I go to see the English doctor dressing Bobomme's wounds. He is charming. Still no refugees.

It seems that Mr. Level has arrived from England. (Handwritten version.)

Mr. Level, R.A.F squadron leader[91] has just arrived from England by plane. (Machine-typed version.)

Two large tanks are parked, one at the back of Clos St Benoît, the other by the entrance gate[92]. The guns thunder incessantly. The residents of Caen are evacuated to Bayeux by the English. Beaufils[93] had his leg blown off in Norrey. Fierce fighting is said to be raging in the streets of Caen, the Hôtel d'Angleterre is on fire. Cherbourg is encircled by the Americans. (Handwritten version.)

Yet, the war continues, the British troops protect the priory with their tanks, and the battle for Caen persists.

We receive candies, chocolate, biscuits, cigarettes, soap. The officers send me some of their white bread. I take a photograph of the captain[94] on the wall and the Canadians[95]. All the soldiers and officers like to show photos of their wives and children. The Germans do the same. How vain and foolish humans are to accept war! (Handwritten version.)
I have just photographed Canadians with Mme Marze in the centre alley, and my friend Captain Hemming astride the garden wall. (Machine-typed version.)
Tonight, I will listen to the news and attend to Bobomme. During the night, sleep interrupted by heavy bombing. But you get used to everything. (Handwritten version.)

Perhaps that's it, the weariness that seems to affect Marcelle Fauchier Delavigne: 'You get used to everything!'

---

91. Officer rank in the Royal Air Force.
92. Refer to the priory map, page 144.
93. Beaufils: former horticultural centre student.
94. See page 154.
95. See page 155.

Wednesday, June 21st

Very bad weather, dark, cold, strong wind. Two tanks are now stationed in Saint-Gabriel: one at the bottom of the Saint-Benoit paddock, the other in front of the entrance barrier. Beaufils, one of our former students, has just lost his leg at Norrey[96]. Furious fighting, we hear, in the streets at Caen. Cherbourg is surrounded by the Americans.

The officers send me some of their white bread. A real treat: I prepare my breakfast in the kitchen while the orderlies make their tea.

Bernard puts all the flowerpots back in the courtyard. (Blue version.)

> 'Normal' life seems to be taking shape: the flowerpots are returned to their usual locations in the courtyard.

A storm is raging. It seems that on the beach the little boats have been wrecked and the tanks damaged. For two days it has been impossible to bring material ashore. The calm and cheerful attitude of the English amazes me.

> From yesterday's events, Marcelle Fauchier Delavigne has retrieved information about the location of the tanks that she deems important to specify. She then focuses on the battles.

Thursday, June 22nd

At half past one I leave for Tracy. The weather is better. Long difficult journey.

I would never have believed it was possible to transform the country so quickly. (Machine-typed version.)

---

96. Norrey: today Saint-Manvieux-Norrey, a village located near Caen, 13 km from Saint-Gabriel.

I have to keep putting my foot down on the ground all the time and have to do it in a cloud of dust. Everywhere there are new tracks. I don't recognize my route. The country is much less closed in: the English knock down walls, open up the hedges. Before coming back, I go to the top of the hill at Arromanches. It is such a beautiful sight that it makes me cry! The barrage balloons shine over me in a very blue sky, the great bridges of boats form jetties and quays in the sea.

Again, her admiration for the British achievements! Marcelle Fauchier Delavigne seems to never tire of this spectacle to which she has already been witness!

When I get back, I learn that five Americans landed here by parachute when their plane caught fire.

One of the captains asks me for the lyrics of Auprès de ma blonde. *We are organizing a concert on Saturday. I am dressing in honour of the English. I eat dinner and then go down to listen to the news. The night is terribly noisy. Constant planes and gun fire. (Handwritten version.)*

A ritual has been established: listening to the news with the English troops.

Friday, June 23rd

There is no mention of this day in the final version. The typed text, however, takes into account the significant influx of refugees from the villages where fighting continues.

The refugees start arriving this morning. Around fifty villagers from Tilly[97], Caumont[98], etc. … Where to accommodate them? All the rooms will be requisitioned, even the barns, the village is overflowing with inhabitants. (Machine-typed version.)

---

97. Tilly: today Tilly-sur-Seulles, located 15 km south of Saint-Gabriel.
98. Caumont: today Caumont-sur-Aure, located 30 km south-west of Saint-Gabriel.

This is the moment when:

Our military has planned to hold a concert tomorrow in the centre courtyard. We are searching for a piano, but there are only two in the area. A platform will be set up on an ox cart in the corner of the courtyard. While it is being prepared, an officer has his hair cut under an apple tree.

Tonight, a visit from Simon, a half-French airman. He is staying in Creully with his squadron and is very popular here because he speaks French admirably. The crowd has grown, now swelled by the presence of all the refugees (new ones are constantly arriving), gathering in front of the priory's door to listen to the news every evening. (Machine-typed version.)

Despite the good weather, a calm night for the first time, and I can finally sleep. (Handwritten version.)

> Here, Marcelle Fauchier Delavigne draws a connection between the clear sky and the nighttime bombings. Could the soldiers adopt the same line of reasoning?

Saturday, June 24th

9am: I go to Creully to get my bicycle repaired and see Mr. Marchal[99].

The post office is handing out interzone cards that we leave at the pharmacy. (Handwritten version.)

… Hoping that they will be carried to their destination by the Red Cross. The pile is already high when I bring mine, and the seemingly sceptical pharmacist tells us that no one has come to pick it up yet. (Blue version.)

I send one to Mano. (Handwritten version.)

---

99. Marchal is a judge in Creully.
100 Interzone card: also known as a family card. It consists of a series of pre-printed formulas and only allows for brief and impersonal news to be given without allowing the correspondent to add a word freely.

Another visit from a motorcyclist from the Military Police. He questions me about the locals. He reassures me about the refugees he is watching over. (Blue version.)

> On the Saturday, in the final version, the information from the previous day regarding the concert, the officer's haircut, and airman Simon's popularity among the Normans are included.

My English friends have decided to give a concert in the courtyard of the Centre tomorrow. A stage will be put up on the bullock cart in the corner of the yard. While the preparations go on an officer is having his hair cut under an apple-tree. This evening the half-French pilot, Simon, comes on a visit. He is at Creully with his squadron and is an immense success here because he speaks French so well. At the time we listen to the news a crowd, enlarged by all the refugees, assembles in front of the priory gate. Preparations for the concert all day, in uncertain weather. My two big flags have the honour of lying on a sheet of camouflage ornamented with bits of brown and green cloth at the back of the stage. In front, all our best geraniums surround the regimental badge[100]. At 4 o'clock, a rehearsal[101]. The 'philosopher' is at the piano. Captain Grose sets himself to reciting the words of 'Auprès de ma blonde' in a strong accent and with charming good humour and little Boucher[102] sings *Ça sent si bon la France*.

At 4 o'clock, rehearsal at the village school. The 'Philosophe' is at the piano, his fingers are very nimble… Too nimble!… like his contradictory mind. He performs a waltz by Faust, then an embellished Si mes vers avaient des ailes… *Poor Reynaldo[103]!…*

Finally, a young beginner brutalises the piano and massacres an unfortunate impromptu tune by Schubert, that had done him no

---

100. See page 156.
101. Concert programme. See page 157.
102. One of the students from the Centre.
103. The music is by the composer and conductor Reynaldo Hahn. He is a friend of Marcelle Fauchier Delavigne's family.

The concert

Among the locals present, we find Monique, the daughter of Philippe Livry-Level, who sought refuge at the Château de Saint-Gabriel. She describes the concert as follows:

'*An event at the Saint-Gabriel Priory was quite instructive. One evening, the army theatre, which naturally followed the troops in the campaign, gave a performance to which the village was invited. The weather was magnificent, the front was particularly silent, and the acts were performed, one after another, amidst general euphoria. Unfortunately, to please the British, the French sang a song by Charles Trenet, provoking an outcry. Charles Trenet was not highly regarded in London, and it was impossible to make the unleashed soldiers understand that not all artists are heroes and that even in wartime, basic needs prevail.*' (Monique Corblet de Fallerans, *Voyage nocture au bout du parc : D'Audrieu à Ravensbrück*, Heimdal Editions, 1994.)

The reliability of this testimony is questionable. The names of the participants are those of the officers' present at the priory and not those of an army theatre troupe... Moniqe Livry-Level lived at the opposite side of the village.

---

harm, tackling it head-on in third gear, pressing the pedal like an accelerator. (Machine-typed version.)

Back home, I find Major Chapman, who tells me that he wants to say a few words in French at the end of the concert. He speaks very little French, the intention is charming, but who will answer him? I run to the castle begging the squadron leader *to do so. He will answer in English. A fairly clear sky with some pink clouds. Planes pass continually over head. (Blue version.)*

8 o'clock. A fairly clear sky, with a few pink clouds. Planes pass continually over our heads, and the guns chase them. The audience is assembled in a semicircle around the stage. On one side the local people sitting on benches [...]

[...] with the refugees (a few couples in the back start dancing when the music allows). (Machine-typed version.)

On the other, all the troops, who laugh, sing, and applaud with magnificent spirit. There are people everywhere, on the steps of the staircase, and at all the small windows round the courtyard. The headquarters officers, all in full dress, pips[104] and buttons shining, are sitting at the door of the refectory, and I am next to them. It is fine. I have a rose in my buttonhole and a grey dress that I have never worn before but kept for the day of their arrival. The guns have not stopped firing, nor have the planes stopped flying over. The noise sometimes drowned the voice of the singers.

Looking up, I catch sight of small white flakes in the sky. The accordion, the bombs, the bagpipes, jazz, the artillery, form the most unexpected, the most moving orchestra!... Dusk is near... In a moment of silence, the toad begins to sing. (Machine-typed version.)

When we stood and heard *God save the king* and the *Marseillaise'*, I felt that I was living through a perfect moment that would die with the day. All night, thunders of artillery, always from the Tilly direction.

> And after this moment of 'peace', the harsh return to reality with the battles around Tilly-sur-Seulles.

Sunday, June 25th

The tanks in the Clos Saint-Benoît left in the night. A large crowd at Mass, many English, the church is too small to take everyone. (Blue version.)

---

104. Pips: British army rank patches, sewn fabric.

A tiring day, continuous traffic of tanks shaking the walls, and loud firing. At 2 o'clock, I hear that our whole headquarters is leaving tomorrow. They are sorry and so am I. One of the captains is already going today.

I passed illustrated postcards out to them, search for any memory that could bring them joy. They promise to come back with their families in times of peace... They will be back much sooner. (Machine-typed version.)

Foin[105] tells me that Pierre de Chevigné[106] is in Bayeux. At 3 o'clock, the kind captain has just left. He shakes my hand. The 'philosopher' is happy to have a copy of "La grandeur du nain[107]".

They are all so kind. The rain is back tonight. An Englishman comes to pick up cabbages and questions me. I've missed the news hour. (Handwritten version.)

Rain in the evening: the capture of Cherbourg is reported[108].

The Allies, they say, have entered Cherbourg; they are now in control of the port!... A huge success, but alas, in our sector, progress is much slower, and the gun fire remains ever so close. (Machine-typed version.)

I sleep in spite of the loud and incessant noise. For the past three weeks we have known no silence. Some people are beginning to lose confidence.

---

105. Foin is a former student at the centre.
106. Pierre de Chevigné is a colonel, a Resistance fighter; he landed in Normandy on June 14, 1944, and is in command of operations at the Bayeux bridgehead.
107. Title of one of the novels written by Marcelle Fauchier Delavigne. "*The Greatness of the Dwarf*".
108. This announcement is a rather premature: the Battle of Cherbourg only coming to an end on June 26. In the presence of the American General Joseph Lawton Collins, the German General Karl von Schlieben signs the surrender of Cherbourg, referred to as the 'Treaty of Servigny', in Yvetot-Bocage (Manche).

Monday, June 26th

Threatening weather, at 6, I go to the padre's last mass. Solitude populated with shadows. A moment that is special in its completeness, too full to last. Getting back, defeatist rumours. I am angry. It is true that the guns seem to be close today but I don't accept what is being said. At 11, I go to have tea in the officers' mess under the porch before they leave. I am rather moved.

The farewell tea! (Machine-typed version.)

Are they, as a service unit, leaving so as to be replaced by fighting soldiers? I can't ask them, so I tell Major Chapman, who is aware that I am responsible for the school and forty boys, that I trust him, and I ask him to warn me if there is anything I ought to do. And then I feel completely calm. He promised me and I feel sure that he will keep his promise. The colonel and Major Chapman have left, all the sections are getting ready to follow them. The lorries are being loaded, to go, I think, to Vaussieux[109] near Bayeux.

> These few lines provide us with some relative precision regarding the role of the soldiers present in the pasture behind the priory: their affiliation with the supply service. However, the name of their regiment is still unknown… Furthermore, we sense growing concern in the words of Marcelle Fauchier Delavigne, who informs us that there are still forty students in the school premises at the time!

They gave me soap, chocolate, plenty of cigarettes, even the white bread made by their cook, and a delicious cake. They are, I believe, heading to Vauxelles[110]. Another visit from my friend from the security service. (Handwritten version.)

---

109. Vaussieux: hamlet of the village of Vaux-sur-Seulles located 3 km from Saint-Gabriel.
110. Vauxelles: this may refer to Vaucelles, a village located west of Bayeux. But in the final version, Marcelle Fauchier Delavigne opts for Vaussieux…

I give him the names of Ami's son and Mme Marze's brother, who are part of the Resistance in Eure and could be useful to him. (Blue version.)

At 4, a walk with Madame Marze in the pasture by the canal. We go along the hedges past all the lorries with the tents in which the men live. They chat with us, always asking about the attitude of the Germans. They are generally very favourable to the Russians, whom they much admire.

We are now in the Clos Saint Benoît. (Blue version.)

Very threatening weather, the storm breaks, we take shelter in a small low tent […]

[…] where we must crawl on the ground to get in. (Blue version.)

And suddenly I feel myself carried far away… to an unknown dream country. Dark, mysterious. The rain drums over our heads. Now I can make out a man lying down… Another offers me a cigarette… At one side a man is singing and playing a guitar.

Superb impression. Is it because I am used to the theatre that I can appreciate the picturesque aspect of a real-life scene so much? Men sing very nostalgic and colonial. They are the 'royal ingeniors[111]*' and the black-berets tank crews who stay there. Pat seems quite at home with the men in the tent. (Handwritten version.)*

> At the Clos Saint-Benoît, another group of soldiers has set up camp: the Royal Engineers, perhaps those responsible for installing the pumping system for the Seulles.

Dinner with the last officer here, Cap. Okins. Very calm night. I believe it's the first full night of sleep in three weeks. (Handwritten version.)

> Exhaustion takes over from her anxiety…

---

111. Royal Engineers, the members of this regiment are called sappers. They are involved in combat engineering, and construction of fortifications, bridges, and roads.

Once again, this is a day that is not mentioned in the final text!

Captain Ocking is still here this morning; he takes a final look, it is a matter of honour for the English army to leave the premises they vacate in a state of order and cleanliness. After a last cup of tea, my young captain is gone. Half an hour later, a visit from Major Chapman, … another cup of tea, and we talk a lot about English and French writers; he is a poet. (Machine-typed version.)

The radio announces a German retreat between Tilly and Caen of around 5 kilometres (M. J. Marie[112] already mentioned it yesterday morning, but in the opposite direction). (Handwritten version.)

At 3 o'clock, despite the wind, rain, and impassable roads, I cycle to Bayeux where I search in vain for a portrait of General de Gaulle, and also his magnificent declaration of June 18th. 'France has lost a battle, but France has not lost the war, etc. …'.

Impossible to find either! … Why? I am told that General de Gaulle does not want to imitate Pétain, who had his portrait displayed everywhere; no comparison, it's not a question of forcing people to have this portrait, but allowing them to find it. It seems that these early French officials are afraid to let the population show their enthusiasm. At the Bayeux sub-prefecture, I offer my services. I am dismissed. (Machine-typed version.)

An airplane has landed in the Buhon[113] field, on the side of the road, like a swallow. Tiring journey, heavy traffic, bad roads, wind, and rain. At the wool merchant's, a portrait of General de Gaulle and the speech he made on June 16, 1940. I congratulate her, but all in all, there is little enthusiasm. (Blue version.)

---

112. Unknown character
113. The castle farmer. His exact name is Buon.

And on the way back, it's my kind English friends who come in large numbers, like every evening, to meet me. I bring them what they all want most: perfume. They want to send it to their wives, and also butter, cheese… The famous camemberts, still unavailable yesterday, are in abundance in all the shops today, but it's not just the gifts they are after; they enjoy talking, asking questions, several would like to learn French. They would gladly chat all night, but I am so tired! …

Tonight, the Americans very kindly bring us a full truck of our refugees who, despite formal prohibition, managed to slip into the enemy lines at Tilly to bring back three rabbits and a few bottles of wine. A corpulent lady jumps into my arms. (Machine-typed version.)

A new Pioneer Major comes to look for accommodation. I show him around. He will come back tomorrow. I reluctantly tear myself away from all these friendly English people, but I am exhausted! I am so tired that I manage to sleep despite the noise. (Blue version.)

Wednesday, June 28th

Weather overcast and uncertain. Arrival of new officers. An old colonel wearing a cartridge belt who laughs like a child and would be totally relaxed confronted by a lion but seems intimidated before a woman. His orderly, a trapezist in civilian life, is very amusing. Heavy, stormy weather. I feel pretty tired.

This terrible, incessant noise constantly shaking the walls is also bound to shake the nerves. I have never so appreciated the value of silence.

An old general comes to admire the Priory. Cap[tain] Optins[114] comes here again this morning.

Oh, how marvelous, this silence is! English soldiers are still coming to ask me for eggs, milk, strawberries. I try to satisfy them. I am

---

114. Could this be Captain Ocking?

called three times over my dinner. It's also to question me about the local folk's opinion. (Handwritten version.)

> Once again, Marcelle Fauchier Delavigne demonstrates her descriptive skills with the portrait she provides of the old colonel! While the strawberries undoubtedly come from her garden in front of the priory, the milk and eggs are to be found in one of the village farms…

At 9 p.m. I slip again into a tent to listen to the news. Two or three of our students are there with English caps on their heads.

There's Touchard and Sebire with English caps on their heads. Durot, Gavet, Berrier[115]. (Handwritten version.)

Details about the taking of Cherbourg, new advances in the Villers-Bocage region and around Caen. The beginning of a big tank battle near Caen, 4 German divisions are said to be marshalled there. Finally the reporter from Normandy gives the latest news and says: 'The happily liberated Normans at Creully are thinking of their brothers who are still prisoners. Gathered round the radio, they listen avidly for news and send their warmest thoughts.' And the Parisians wonder about us, perhaps also gathered round the radio.

And Mano must hear about this. (Handwritten version.)

> We are unaware if the message from the inhabitants of Creully relayed by the BBC could have been heard by the Parisians, which include her husband.

Very noisy night, furious firing. It is no doubt the battle that was foretold.

---

115. Some of the students.

Another day that is not included in the final text, but by compiling the different versions, we obtain a set of complementary information.

A day pretty much like the ones before. I'm going to Creully. All the roads are changing. A lot of them are unrecognisable. (Handwritten version.)

At the top of the hill, a plane is landing in front of me like a bird. (Blue version.)

The wall by the canal has collapsed. (Handwritten version.)

The English need stones to rebuild the roads and fill in the ditches. (Machine-typed version.)

In the morning, the officer comes to apologise. Tracks criss-cross in all directions on the grass. (Handwritten version.)

Several visits tonight. They come to get butter, cheese, bread and, above all, to talk. Two of them sit in the room and talk for 2 hours. Big storm and heavy gunfire through the night. (Handwritten version.)

Clearly, respect for private property has been somewhat neglected. The wall delimiting the canal pasture has been destroyed, beautiful old stones from the Creully quarry are used to fill in the roads and ditches, and the pasture is no more than a walking path. The damage having been done, an officer comes to apologise, and Marcelle Fauchier Delavigne – who shares her food and her time with them – clearly accepts…

The Hotel du Lion d'Or, a former post house that became the journalists' headquarters

Gustave Bessières, who already owned a hotel in Mayenne, purchased this 17th-century former post house in 1928, undertaking extensive work in it up to 1932. He decided to split the building at 73 rue Saint-Jean in two to create a proper alley between the street and the hotel. His wife, Augustine, was a cooker and was rapidly awarded one of the very first *Michelin Guide* stars.

Immediately following the Normandy Landings, the Lion d'Or became the press headquarters. Ernest Hemingway and Robert Capa were among its residents. But war correspondents were not the hotel's only visitors – Maurice Schumann also stayed there.

Friday, June 30th

Very uncertain weather. I go to lunch in Bayeux. A plane is lying in front of me on the edge of the road.

> Here, Marcelle Fauchier Delavigne takes liberties with the chronology of events by assigning yesterday's plane episode to this day…

The Hotel du Lion d'Or is overflowing with allied troops. I see Americans for the first time, guns on their backs, butts upward. The comings and goings, the disturbance in this usually very peaceful hotel, are unimaginable. It is almost impossible to get served. A very light lunch, but very interesting, opposite a young French pilot in the American army.

We gather in front of the press release: the cars come in, go out. The dining room is buzzing. (Machine-typed version.)

> This is the hotel where Emmanuel and Marcelle Fauchier Delavigne stayed in the winter, when they came to the

garden Centre, for central heating was only installed in their house in 1971.

The road is like a river of khaki flowing from top to bottom. The town is unrecognizable.

Colored men[116] are laughing, showing their white teeth. (Handwritten version.)

> Marcelle Fauchier Delavigne describes what she sees with words that would not be accepted nowadays… on the subject of American soldiers, words that she censored in the final version.

At the subprefecture in Chevigné. (Handwritten version.)

At the billeting office of the allied armies I see a poster advertising for an English-speaker. I offer my services: Major Jerry, very friendly, engages me at once. I begin work on Monday, I am delighted, I have a job. Very noisy night, 21 Boche planes shot down.

> The Allied armies' billeting office have replaced the German Army billeting office at 10 rue Saint-Malo[117].

Saturday, July 1st

> This day does not appear in the final text. The handwritten version allowed for these few lines to be drafted in the blue version:

The weather is still quite bad. Nothing special happened today. I bring a few roses to the English soldiers' graves. Madame Marze is going to Bayeux in Father Bouillet's[118] carriole [crossed-out line]. It will take a while! but I heard that by passing through the fields, it is possible. I tried to read this afternoon, to no avail, an active

---

116. In the original text, Marcelle Fauchier Delavigne uses an offensive word, now widely considered racist.
117. See page 159.
118. Bouillet was a saddler and occupied a farm at the crossroads of the Fresnay road and the Creully road in Rucqueville.

occupation would be better, I will have one on Monday. Heavy rain tonight. (Blue version.)

With the exception of the nationality of the soldiers' graves, this could have been an ordinary day under a Norman sky!

Sunday, July 2nd

Gunfire all night long. Cloudy weather. This morning, the church is full of people: even more soldiers, even more refugees and the Normans struggle to get inside. ... Over lunch, a new formation arrives. An officer from the Intelligent [sic] Service[119] asks for housing. I offer him what's left. And here is Captain Ocking, coming to get his laundry, always polite and cheerful. In the pasture, a few heavily damaged tanks come back from the front. We are turning into a repair park. In the evening, we have several visits and my friends never come empty-handed: only wonderful things, impossible to find, come out of their pockets! ... bars of soap, cigarettes, chocolate, sardines, etc. ... They come to sit, and we chat. A very sweet feeling of amicable union. (Machine-typed version).

Intelligence Service

The Secret Intelligence Service (SIS), also known as MI6 (Military Intelligence, section 6), is the foreign intelligence service of the United Kingdom. It is made up of Field Security Officers (FSO) who are tasked with enemy counterespionage, countersabotage and counterpropaganda operations on the battlefield.

---

119. The Intelligence Service set up its headquarters in the Sommervieu seminar, on the outskirts of Bayeux.

This day also completely disappears from the final text. There is nothing new to the life that has progressively taken shape within the priory: the soldiers' presence at Mass, a request for accommodation, visitors who bring sweets and chat. And yet, there is one detail on the activity in the pasture, now used as a reception and repair centre for tanks!

Monday, July 3rd

Awful weather, rain. At half past eight this morning I go to have a little real coffee with Madame Marze before leaving for Bayeux on my bicycle. I arrived soaked at the billeting office. The major is pleased to see me, the French worker much less so. The premises are in a pitiful state. A filthy house, rickety stairs, no light, a table and a few chairs. My job, it seems, is to go round workshops. A motor-cycle is needed as the motor-cyclist has been killed on the way. The major asks if I know how to use one? Alas, no! But I can offer my car. I shall work, I think, with Lieutenant Fraser, a cold boy, a little mysterious, with long, half-closed Asiatic eyes.

> This is Marcelle Fauchier Delavigne's first day at 'work' and, clearly, the setting does not look like much. Indeed, the English billeting office had been set up in the same premises as those used by the Germans for their own office!

Cap. Opkins[120] finds me in my old shop, in one of the oldest houses in Bayeux. I think that the Englishman is somewhat shocked. (Handwritten version.)

> The machine-typed version specifies that she goes to visit the construction sites:

They are everywhere (levelling works, ammunition that piles up like walls along the hedges and rises in pyramids under the apple trees). So much work produced by this relentless hive. Just the cleaning of all the machine cogs and crate locks, which had to be coated with a product or stuffed with waterproof cloth, is

---

120. The captain's name certainly allows for spelling interpretations!

such prodigious work? The troops are not enough, they need some French manpower. (Machine-typed version.)

There is still much bustle at the Lion d'Or. The courtyard is full of cars. The press, in particular, is installed there. I read the communiqué announcing the arrival of 11 German divisions! … I dry myself with difficulty. There is no fire anywhere, and after copying names and figures in the office records, I get back to Saint-Gabriel frozen. At 7 o'clock Major Jerry is already there to look at the car. He seems delighted. What a triumph to have been able to hide this car from the Bosches so as to be able to offer it to the English… The mechanic will come tomorrow to get it going again.

> We discover what we would now refer to as her job description: copying names and figures and going to construction sites, but to do so, she needs a means of transport other than the bicycle she uses to come to Bayeux. Marcelle Fauchier Delavigne generously offers the car she hid during the German occupation, and that now needs a service after all this time! This section also informs us that this modern and independent woman has a driving licence.

Still many visits tonight. I give cheese, butter, eggs and receive chocolate, sweets, sardines, cigarettes and matches, they all come to sit down in the room. Fairly quiet night. (Handwritten version.)

Tuesday, July 4th

At 9 a.m I leave for Bayeux. Better weather. The major wants cups, plates, spoons. He doesn't suspect that all this is unobtainable. I go to consult my friend Madame Métais, the antique dealer[121]. The poor major is sleeping on a board. She is willing to provide him with a mattress and offers her own cups.

---

121. Her shop was located in rue des Bouchers.

The major's lodgings, in a disgusting old room, consist of a plank and a blanket. Madame Métais can find a mattress. Lunch at the Lion d'Or, then shopping in Bayeux with the major (Handwritten version.)

> Taking notes, Marcelle Fauchier Delavigne specifies that the Major's name is 'Jerry', without providing any information on his regiment…

During the day, go round different stores and yards with Lieutenant Fraser. We go to Saint-Côme, then Asnelles[122]…, poor Asnelles…, what destruction! There is very little left of anything, a gate, a wall, a villa, even people! And yet it is people who have done all this!… Is it magnificent or monstrous? … Rattling around in the jeep, we go through hedges, crash into potholes, climb up banks. Fine, confident, sturdy lads drive us through all these camps and all this equipment, astonishing in its quantity. I bicycle home from Bayeux, unable to do more. I fall into bed and sleep, whatever the noise.

> On this evening, Marcelle Fauchier Delavigne ponders on subjects she will also consider later, and they demonstrate her inner questioning: 'I think that to build, you have to destroy.'

Wednesday, July 5th

What a good sleep… I feel better. I have this morning off. Sandals and slacks (*pyjama*). Fine weather. Sunshine. Walk in the garden with the comical clown. He has been round the world. And left a girl-friend in every continent? He knows about botany as well as the sea, poetry as well as explosives. He dizzies me with fantastic stories and goes off bouncing like a rubber ball.

I inform the major that I don't feel strong enough to bicycle every day to work, he says that he will send for me. (Handwritten version.)

---

122. Saint-Côme – more precisely Saint-Côme-de-Fresné – and Asnelles are two villages located around ten kilometres from Saint-Gabriel.

The BBC

At the time, it had almost been a month since the BBC set up a studio in the small town of Creully, less than 3 kilometres to the east of Saint-Gabriel. It followed a request from General Montgomery whose headquarters were established at the foot of the Château de Creully, in the grounds of the Château de Creullet. The task of setting up the first studio in liberated France was entrusted to Frank Gillard (1908-1998), a British war correspondent who worked for the BBC. At first, he set up his equipment under a tent, but the noise of the ongoing combat was too loud, and he needed to find a different location. It was to be the square tower at the fortified Château de Creully, the thick walls of which offered a soundproofed studio. Here, for weeks, dozens of reporters cut their reports and bulletins on recording devices and the discs were flown to London in the late afternoon from the airfields in Bazenville-Crépon and Lantheuil. Broadcast in the evening, they were translated in around fifty different languages, and we can safely say that this small studio in the countryside became one of the most visited and the most important radio production centres in the world in the summer of 1944.

After housing a Radio Museum for many years, from which amateur radios were broadcast, the square tower is now home to a BBC museum that officially opened on June 6th 2019.

Afternoon, in Bayeux again. The road is arduous. The Major tells me that he will send a car for me… He has got his cups, teapot, etc. … Thanks to Madame Métais and not without a great deal of pain for me. He does not know about the scarcity nor the price of these objects. I spent 275 F[123], and when I mention 50 F, he thinks

---

123. The French currency at the time was the French franc (sign: F or FF).

that it is a reasonable price… On the way back, two BBC war correspondents stop by. They would like six bedrooms. I lead them to the Château, the only place in the village that might still have some. Madame Level announces that she has run out of rooms. … I go next door to the Buhon's. The farm is full… This evening, an Englishman tells me that during the landings, many French people shot at them… What to do to get rid of such shame… (Blue version.)

Here comes the whole Intelligent [sic] Service group. Tents are pitched in the courtyard of the priory and behind the big lime tree. About ten lorries and cars are camouflaged under the apple trees, not an inch of the land is left unused. The officers are friendly, sociable-looking people who master French admirably, but who seem neither military nor English. (Machine-typed version.)

This evening Major Hodgson comes back to ask for bedrooms for his staff. I offer him the room where we have tea and where there is a divan. It is all I have left. Going near the river, I stop, amazed. The English have set up machines on the bank which pump up and purify the water and deliver it into tankers that take it to the armies. They are trying to preserve life rather than destroy it. This is one of the strongest impressions I have of the English army.

> The machine-typed version offers a more detailed descrip-
> tion of this pumping activity:

On the river bank, the English have set up machines which pump up water, and they transfer it to big tanks where it is purified, and tankers drive continuously through the pasture to be filled with this drinking water to take it to the army. (Machine-typed version.)

> In Saint-Gabriel, water is also pumped in the pastures. The
> English even go as far as setting up a permanent pumping
> station on the other end of the village, which is still known
> today as 'La bâtisse aux Anglais[124]'.

---

124. See village map page 143.

La bâtisse aux Anglais

The Saint-Gabriel pumping station, known as the *'bâtisse aux Anglais'*, was built by the Pioneers from the 222nd Company and the Sappers from the 653rd Road Construction Company, both part of the 13th Airfield Construction Group (ACG). It comprised four pumps, one of which was transferred to Creully after the Second World War. The station supplied the airfields in Coulombs, aka B-6, and Lantheuil, aka B-9. It also had settling tanks for drinking water.

Each Sulzer-brand pump had a flow rate of 100,000 litres per hour. Together, every night, they produced close to 15 million litres of water at the airfields. Their Hercules engines had been bought and tested by the British Army as early as 1943. All this equipment, transported by Dakota planes from England to Coulombs, was in service on July 15th, 1944. One of these pumps, taken from Saint-Gabriel, is still operational today at the Creully firefighters' emergency pumping station.

Built on a concrete slab, pumps and engines were protected out of water in rustic buildings which were built of hewn stone, sourced from nearby quarries, and covered: the roof cladding at Saint-Gabriel is made of a combination of planks that were originally used to pack the engines. They still bear their identification and control numbers.

From these four stations, pipes of 10 to 15 cm (4 to 6 inches) in diameter distributed water to the five dusty airfields. These kilometres of pipeline stretched across the countryside and the roads, sometimes buried in trenches, sometimes suspended like aerial walkways. This nighttime irrigation finally allowed the soil to be sufficiently soaked with water to control the dust throughout the following day.

(According to research by Philippe Bauduin.)

Thursday, July 6th

Once more, this day does not appear in the final version...
The machine-typed version omits insignificant details...
Such as the Intelligence Service setting up in the courtyard
(apparently much to Marcelle Fauchier Delavigne's delight),
a few students running away, the bombing of Caen...

This morning, mass is said for Jean. I am off work today. Still looking for accommodation for English newcomers. The whole Intelligent [sic] Service group is here now. They pitched up tents in the central courtyard and behind the big lime tree and settled there[125]. About ten lorries and cars are parked beneath the apple trees. They are friendly, sociable-looking people who master French admirably, but who seem neither military nor English. (Blue version.)

Thunderstorm and artillery. A lot of noise, no sleep. This morning, it is raining, but it doesn't last. Major Hodgson[126] accepted my proposal, he will stay in the room with his Colonel, the other officers will camp under the tent. At Banville[127] near the 'air field' [sic] where Dakota planes bring supplies every day, and leave with the seriously injured who arrive in England an hour and a half later. (Machine-typed version.)

I go to Creully for supplies amidst a swarm of vehicles. On the way back, I meet a trapeze artist who likes to talk politics. A socialist, with no illusions about a possible improvement. He laughs, gets a kick out of everything, even out of his colonel. Weird man, not dumb. He knew Blum[128] whom he admires. At 5 o'clock, Major Jerry arrives from Bayeux with his colonel. They come to see the car. The colonel, joyful, bon vivant, *announces the arrival of the English in Paris in 15 days. Here comes Major Hoghson too, from the first formation, asking me if I can house their headquarters*

---

125. See priory map page 144.
126. Or Hogson? The spelling of proper nouns varies from day to day...
127. See map of the area around Saint-Gabriel page 143, Banville is located 9 km northeast of Saint-Gabriel.
128. Léon Blum: a French socialist statesman, 1872-1950.

once again. What should I do? I have no free space left. I offer him the room where we have tea, which has a divan. He will talk about it to his colonel. (Blue version.)

While I am having dinner with the officers, Madame Marze calls for me: three students have made off – Frantz, Bonnefoy and Pelletier. They are sure to be camping in some nearby meadow while enjoying English canned food with the troops.

Tonight, a cloud of English bombers passes over us and fills the whole red sky: rumbling, droning, bursting; thunder accompanies this extraordinary spectacle, everyone, eyes raised, we never tire of admiring these birds as they come in tight masses, as more, and more again, follow them, dense purple clouds concealing them from time to time… And the next day, we learn that Caen just suffered its most appalling air raid… It will be the last. (Machine-typed version)

Friday, July 7th

The information provided yesterday in the various versions are summarised on July 7th.

A storm and guns firing. A lot of noise tonight. In the morning it is raining but it doesn't last. The colonel has agreed to my suggestion. He will sleep in the tea-room with one of his officers (generally Major Chapman). The others will be in tents at Banville next to an 'air field' [sic] where Dakotas land every day with supplies and leave with the seriously wounded, who will be in England in an hour and a half.

Dinner with the officers. During dinner Madame Marze calls me out to tell me that three students have made off: Frantz, Bonnefoy, and Pelletier. They are sure to be camping in meadows with the troops.

A cloud of English bombers goes over, filling the whole red sky. A very beautiful sight. A deafening drone. Terrible night. Incessant bombardments, impossible to sleep.

The major's driver arrives from Bayeux to fix my car. It is rather harrowing to sit once more on this red leather! The car is looking good. They all admire it. (Handwritten version.)

Marcelle Fauchier Delavigne's car is worthy of these few lines.

Saturday, July 8th

The radio announces today that the English are at the gates of Caen.

In the final version, this single line summarises the entire text below!

Fine weather. At 8 a.m., I get picked up from Bayeux. This time, it is the discreet Frayser[129] himself who drives me in my car. He is disappointed, me too. He hoped that we would use this car for our work, but it has charmed the colonel who wants to make it his personal vehicle. If only it were just the car that had charmed him! … but the little accountant who works at the refugee office seems to have done the same and Frayser is even less approving.

Tonight, I am driven back in the rain in the major's car by a driver who speaks Cockney and reminds me of Nelly[130]. He told me: 'If I had a car like yours, I'd never be able to part with it.' The English deserve for me to make this sacrifice for them.

As soon as I get back, I lecture the students. They are unbearable. Pierson lit up a rocket in the dormitory and almost set it on fire.

One of the Intelligent [sic] Service officers gives me a journal published in London. La France Libre. *Such indescribable delight it is*

---

129. Frayser or Fraser is one of the English officers.
130. We are unable to identify this Nelly with certainty, she could be Nelly de Vogüé, Saint-Exupéry's muse. She and Marcelle Fauchier Delavigne had a common friend named Louise de Vilmorin.

to read these well-written articles which openly declare what has been choking us for 4 years! Tonight, the radio announces that the English are at the gates of Caen. (Blue version.)

Sunday, July 9th

A lot of people at mass. I had difficulty finding a seat, a lot of soldiers taking communion. Then I go for a walk with Pat across the pastures to the fir-wood. Very fine work. The hillside is transformed. They have knocked things down. They have opened things up. They have demolished. They have made roads. It is a different landscape, but still a very beautiful landscape. Mediocre weather. There is a light drizzle. Great emotion in listening to the news. Caen has been taken by the Canadians and English. Night is a little quieter.

> In fact, only the left bank of the River Orne has been evacuated by the Germans and freed, de facto, by the English and Canadian troops. The fighting in the capital of Basse-Normandie (Lower Normandy) will last another ten days. The liberation of the right bank by the Canadians, on July 19th, will barely be mentioned by Marcelle Fauchier Delavigne in her text.

They are trying to preserve life rather than destroy it. This is one of the strongest impressions I have of the English army. (Blue version.)

This observation was not included in the published edition, despite its philosophical dimension.

Monday, July 10th

Today I work in a big pasture on the Littry[131] road. The English are going to establish a camp where they will store all the army's supplies of clothing, boots etc. First the tents have to be erected. I have the job of explaining the work to some local countrywomen. It is raining in torrents. We splash about in the grass all day; I get back to Saint-Gabriel soaked. At 6 o'clock a French lesson for a young captain.

Today I work in a big pasture on the Littry road, next to the cemetery[132]. (Machine-typed version.)

Several supply camps for the British Army had been set up near the D-Day Landing beaches. The exact location of this one cannot be determined.

At the office in Bayeux, arrival of an 'interpreter' who is exactly like Tristan Bernard[133]. The major threw him out. Really comical. Very bad weather tonight. Quiet night, good sleep. (Handwritten version.)

---

131. Littry: today, this village is called Le Molay-Littry, since it merged in 1969 with the village of Le Molay. It is located 15 km west of Bayeux.
132. This may refer to the old west cemetery, which has since been moved.
133. Tristan Bernard (1866-1947) was a novelist and a playwright.

Tuesday, July 11th

Weather a bit better, I go back to the camp near Bayeux. Several tents are now up so we shall have shelter if it rains. Today the women have the job of sorting the washing and clothes that have come back from the front. Proud of their organization, the English explain all that they plan to do there? Very interesting to follow this admirably conceived plan.

Here, the arrival of lorries, bringing clothes back from the front that are immediately sorted: some are to be burnt, others are to be mended, others only need to be washed. Further away, the shops for new items. Between the two: repair lorries, a genuine shoe repair workshop that has the latest techniques, another with sewing machines... and what sewing machines! the best nickel-plated models that shine like mirrors. And to say that all these things crossed the Channel... And each lorry is equipped with wireless telegraphy. Meticulous attention to detail goes hand in hand with overall perfection. The Normans who will be tasked to carry out the work are petrified with admiration. (Machine-typed version.)

They bring me to the landowner's and always come looking for me to talk to a worker. I feel useful. I love it. (Blue version.)

I feel really useful here between the very nice English and the friendly workers. A lot of tents have already been put up. The subprefecture does nothing for the refugees. A lot will arrive from liberated Caen. English lesson and dinner with the officers. (Handwritten version.)

> Marcelle Fauchier Delavigne had found a meaning to her days, a place where she can practice her skills, in particular thanks to her mastery of the English language.

On my return I find the Centre in commotion. Durot was able to bicycle as far as Caen and what he saw there is terrifying. The town no longer exists! He wasn't able to find out anything about his parents who lived in the Vaucelles area, on the right bank of the Orne, which he could not get to, as the Boches still occupy part of it.

No news from Madame Marze's daughter, the house where she lived on Rue Saint-Pierre is still standing, but the doors are broken and the flat is empty. (Machine-typed version.)

Major pages in history became part of everyday life. Caen was only 20 kilometres away, but the town was not yet liberated – only the left bank at this point in time.

The old pioneer major told me that he received a notice from Bayeux to drive me every day to the billeting office, it's wonderful. Some explosions tonight. (Handwritten version.)

Wednesday, July 12th

Overcast. The stone bench in the garden, beneath the walnut tree, is the RASC Colonel and Major Chapman's washroom. I must look out the window, before going out, to make sure that they are not using it. (Machine-typed version.)

Cohabiting with the officers sometimes requires a great deal of tact.

Like yesterday, I go back to the English camp, but today the weather is nice. Planes are buzzing above us. As soon as I arrive, the camp's lieutenant rushes towards me and asks me to explain to a young blonde woman who accompanies him that she will be a 'team leader'. He repeats several times, 'team leader'. He seems excited. The young blonde woman laughs. This is certainly not the first time she has done this. I go back home in a jeep from the camp. Quiet evening. A bit of rest. (Machine-typed version.)

The women say that they thought I would be the team leader! In the morning, I have a lot of work; in the evening, I can sit down in the grass and read Major Chapman's book of poems, very interesting. (Handwritten version.)

The Royal Army Service Corps (RASC)

This is the British Army corps responsible for land, coastal and lacustrine transport, air shipment, barracks management, the army fire department, the supply of headquarter units, food, water, fuel and household material supply, such as clothing, furniture and stationery, and the supply of technical and military equipment.

Friday, July 14th

The national holiday. I stay at Saint-Gabriel. This morning the two big French and English flags are flying on the tower. At midday, with all the students, and accompanied by Bernard Gavet and Durot, we go to put flowers on the English graves, and then on to the war memorial, where they sing the Marseillaise.

The arrival of 150 refugees from Caen is announced. (Machine-typed version.)

Quite fine weather today. Great battles in the air which we follow from the garden with Captain Hemming. Fascinating. Seven Boche planes shot down. Very strange to see the plane caught between all the salvoes of an anti-aircraft fire and trying in vain to escape.

[…] like a moth to a flame. (Machine-typed version.)

Poetry comes back at the most unexpected moments!

A lot of aircraft passing over tonight. Captain Hemming, whose camp-bed is by the window, got shrapnel from a bomb on his pillow.

We had visitors from morning to night. Army lorries and trailers of refugees coming, often from very far away, to get vegetables. We are now well known.

A refugee talks about a place near Caen that made shells and never got bombed: 'It's because it is an anonymous company,' he says, 'capitalists from every country!' Capitalists! … They really seem to be responsible for the wars, yet there had been wars before them? None of the Englishmen I see seems to be much of a socialist. What should I think of it? What should I believe? I wish I could close my eyes and only see poets! (Handwritten version.)

> Here we can sense Marcelle Fauchier Delavigne's dismay at these statements she cannot control. However, she still has great faith in human nature.

And here is M. Demarais, the first inhabitant of Caen to reappear, a little pale, emotional, shaken. He spent 5 weeks in a cellar. Before the Germans left they stole all the cars and bicycles to get away on.

> M. Desmarais was in charge of the Wards of the Nation[134] in Caen; the garden Centre must have housed some of them. He spent these weeks in his wife's company.

The town caught fire at the beginning of the attack on June 6th. The hardest bombardment came on July 7th. The evening when we were admiring the mass of planes in the red sky. The town was taken the next day.

While the unfortunate inhabitants of Caen were falling under the showers of machine gun fire, we were admiring the many planes in the red sky. That evening, not one single street was passable in the whole town, one of the aims of these bombardments was to make it impossible for reinforcements to pass. The next day, the English

---

134. Ward of the Nation (*Pupille de la Nation*) is a French civil status allocated by the State to those who have a parent injured or killed at war, during a terrorist attack or while carrying out certain public duties.

still managed to enter the town, thanks to their prodigious machines which cleared the way! All our friends from the prefecture: Robiquet[135], Bienfait, Sorel, are safe and sound, but the director of agricultural services, M. Lebot, is very seriously injured and three of his children were killed! (Machine-typed version.)

> These few lines give us two types of information. The first is on how the garden Centre is run. We learn that it maintained a good relationship with the prefecture services and that Marcelle Fauchier Delavigne kept a close eye on its activities because she refers to Madame Robiquet, Bienfait, Sorel and even Lebot as 'friends'. The second is about the Battle for Caen, offering proof that points of view can differ, depending on where you are. What was perceived from afar to be a beautiful spectacle was in fact the beginning of a huge bombardment.

Dinner alone with Major Hodgson. Very friendly, the gentle giant. He likes to speak a mix of French and Spanish and is happy to go to Paris to spend the night in Montmartre. Loud gunfire. (Blue version.)

Sunday, July 16th

There is now mass at 9 o'clock said by Father Tolmer, a cousin of the Roussels who took refuge here. Happy to no longer attend this high-mass where you have to fight to get in! (Blue version.)

With some English and refugees. (Handwritten version.)

Very sultry weather. We take refuge with Pat in the pastures along the river, behind the mill. It is the only place in Saint-Gabriel where the grass is still at all green. The dust has become a real scourge. I did not think it could reach this level. All the trees, all the roofs, all the fields are covered with it; we eat it; good glasses alone can protect the eyes. The banks are chalk white; it is oppressive!

---

135. Robiquet: a prefecture official. He knew all the departmental advisors.

The Men's Abbey (Abbaye-aux-Hommes) in the Battle for Caen

The building that now houses Caen's town hall was, in the summer of 1944, part of a medical compound which also included the Bon-Sauveur civil hospital, the law court and the La Visitation monastery. Thousands of people took refuge here, and the Malherbe secondary school was the most important shelter, with people filling every space – the classrooms, the corridors, the dining hall. Even if red crosses were placed on the school rooftop, they did not prevent the bombardments from claiming victims, for twenty or so were killed.

Today M. Fox[136] arrives, the impeccable M. Fox, our horticulture teacher. He is hardly recognizable! … thin, haggard, collarless, hair hanging loose, a white-painted helmet on the back of his bicycle; he tells us about the taking of the town. The Abbaye aux Hommes and the secondary school are still standing, but the Germans are now trying to get at these two monuments, which are the principal refuge of the inhabitants!

[…] The church has already been hit by a shell. The Abbaye-aux-Dames is also unscathed. The town is still virtually uninhabitable, constantly under German gunfire. (Blue version.)

He seems very moved, asks if we can let his mother stay. His impression of the new leaders from Bayeux is exactly the same as mine. A new trick of the Vichy Fratelli[137] with the Cross of Lorraine. But still Vichy. I am filled with rage. M. Fox says the leaders in Caen are fine. Beautiful fireworks at around 11 p.m. (Handwritten version.)

---

136. See his memories page 135.
137. *Fratelli*: 'brothers' in Italian.

This is one of the rare occasions on which Marcelle Fauchier Delavigne clearly states her aversion for the Vichy regime and the political upheavals that have become apparent since the start of the country's liberation…

Gunfire this evening. (Handwritten version).

Monday, July 17th

Fine weather haze; the wind is from the north, a good direction. I see Major Hodgson washing on the stone bench.

Leave for Bayeux at 8. I am going to be interpreter for an officer who is going to get the town's cold-store, which is in a very bad state, going again…

Lunch at the Lion d'Or, where I meet our nice Scottish doctor again with a charming RAF nurse in the grey-blue uniform and cap of the airmen. She is tall, dark, laughs readily, and is called Miss Hood[138]. I hope they will come to dinner at Saint-Gabriel tomorrow. Visit to the lorries at the Littry camp. In some of them rows of sewing-machines of the best model are installed; in others everything that is needed for shoe repairs. There is a radio in each

---

The cold-store of Bayeux

It was located in Impasse de l'Islet, a cul-de-sac on the banks of the Aure, in a building that had known another useful vocation. In the 19th century, it became a cold-store. Ice packs were made here by pumping water up from the river to cool it in brine. The ice was used under the nearby fish market, in the building that now houses the tourist office. This cold-store where the people of Bayeux came to buy their ice remained open up to the 1960s.

---

138. Kay Hood was a nurse during the war, and she kept in touch with the Fauchier Delavigne family up to her death at 100. See pages 159-160.

lorry. Perfect care about every detail completes the perfection of the whole thing.

All the women ask me to come back and offer me a tour of the sewing-machines in the shoemaker's workshop. I go back to the office where the Major refuses a girl f[or] the hospital after giving her a very comical look. He leads me out and explains everything to me. I didn't know that the Eng[lish] could be like that, or at least not as much as the French are. (Handwritten version.)

Hitchhike home. While I am waiting at the outskirts of Bayeux, a fleet of cars goes past towards Caen, carrying first-aid and Red Cross workers etc.

I have a letter authorising me to get into English cars. While I wait just outside Bayeux for a policeman to pick me up, I'm astonished and overwhelmed at the number of cars heading for Caen (Machine-typed version.)

In one of them I see an old nun who has a tin hat perched on top of her wimple!

On my way back, I find M. Sorel, his mother and his daughter, and Mlle Delain from the Caen prefecture, who have come to seek refuge: their houses have been destroyed, they have absolutely nothing left. For five weeks they have been living in the basements under the school, fortunately the Centre is large and Mme Marze has little trouble finding room even where space is scarce (Machine-typed version.)

I now have dinner every evening with the colonel and Major Chapman, and each time I have to accept whisky, although I have a horror of it: 'just a very little… for France, for Paris.' How can I refuse? After dinner, walking with Pat, I see the remains of the plane that crashed several days ago in the canal pasture. All the tanks have gone. Loud guns tonight, the house shakes. I think that a big offensive has begun.

I dine with the RASC colonel and Major Chapman. (Machine-typed version.)

Tuesday, July 18th

Very fine weather. The sky is full of planes. Flying Fortresses, all white, shine in the sky. One is hit, 9 parachutes come down, our eyes follow their descent. One has landed on the plain[139], I pass it on the way to Bayeux, going back with the English soldiers.

At the billeting office there is always a great stream of workers and a lot of work. I hear that Mr Churchill[140] has just gone along the road, past our door. Hitchhike home once more, this time in a jeep. Charming but what dust! …

I love this classy little car, but dear how much dust it kicks up! (Machine-typed version.)

> When going over this passage again, Marcelle Fauchier Delavigne preferred to speak about the convenience of travelling by jeep, even though the dust taints the memory, rather than highlighting its "classy" aspect, which is less in touch with the time period …

At 7 the young captain comes for his French lesson. Half an hour later I hear a jeep come into the yard. It is the doctor and nice Kay Hood who are coming to dinner with me. A very agreeable evening. A fairly noisy night.

I hope they will come to visit again. (Handwritten version.)

Wednesday, July 19th

This morning, a soldier and friend of Mme Marze brought her a note written by one of the runaway pupils, which he had found near the bridge. Thanks to this, policemen soon brought back Frantz and Bonnefoy, both looking very sheepish. Pelletier is still missing. (Blue version.)

---

139. This large 22-acre field on the road to Bayeux, named 'Madago', was cultivated by the Garden Centre.
140. This was during his second visit to Normandy; during the first, on 13 June 1944, he went to Creullet.

A happy ending to their escapade!

I spend the whole day in Bayeux with an unfortunate woman whose husband and daughter were killed near Saint-Lô. She sobs. She wants to go back there. Very difficult. I get English drivers, who don't know how to refuse anything to a woman in tears, to give her a seat in a lorry going to that area.

She had fainted and was transported to Bayeux to receive medical care, Bayeux being the only city in the region which had not been destroyed. Now, the poor woman is begging to be brought back home. (Machine-typed version.)

On the way back, in rue St Malo, I meet Berty Gillou[141], naval officer and now delegate to the protection of historical monuments. In the office there is a great stir. Major Jerry fired the French employee in charge of hiring workers: I think he was too involved with the pretty blonde, the young accountant and with a young recruit from Formigny. Always smoking a cigarette, he told funny but rude stories. He has been replaced by a big ruddy-faced moron, who speaks English like Tristan Bernard's interpreter[142], and mumbles things like 'It'll come back...'. (Handwritten version.)

This episode, which was taken out from the final version, lacks this short description of a character that easily allowed the reader to imagine him, and which highlighted Marcelle Fauchier Delavigne's writing talents.

The major announces military landings in Dieppe and in Marseille.

Nobody else knows anything about this. Is it true?[143]. We meet with the short Resistance fighter from Marseille and his wife. I visit the

141. Berty Gillou: Albert Gilou, also nicknamed 'Bertie', was a collector, engaged in Free France in December 1942, an officer in the Marine Nationale (French Navy), an interpreter, and communications officer. After the war, he married Blaise Cendrars' daughter, Miriam, and became creative director of the magazines *Réalités* and *Connaissance des arts*.
142. From the play *L'Anglais tel qu'on le parle* (1899) by Tristan Bernard, centred around misunderstandings caused by an interpreter's poor English skills.
143. They were only rumours. Marseille was freed on August 28th and Dieppe on September 1st.

old antique dealer on the road to Littry[144]. *What a curious little house. (Handwritten version.)*

Lots of French officers come to visit our 'Intelligent [sic] service'. They arrive from London, with a briefcase tucked under their arm, looking elegant, mysterious, distant as they ignore us entirely. What a contrast it makes with the charming English politeness! One of them, Captain Ledoux, a short and protective blond man, is introduced by Major Johnson. (Machine-typed version.)

> There seems to be at least one amiable French officer among those she meets, but she visibly prefers the kindness the Englishmen have towards her!

Thursday, July 20th

Fine weather this morning, but the dust and fog combine to make a thick curtain.

At 9 I go round Bayeux with Frederick the trapezist to try to get some wine. The pioneer colonel is having important superior officers to dinner this evening and would like to offer them wine. I once again get Madame Métais interested in my objective. Frederick kisses her hands. Despite the difficulties we get hold of two bottles! …

> It seems important to highlight that rationing measures were still active, that not everything was available and that, not so long before that, the black market was the only way to access this type of goods!

Work in the office, dinner with the officers.

On the way back, Périais[145] *and his friend come to the office. The new guy is the ridiculous and big 'interpreter' … The young woman from Formigny brings a bit of joy. The Lion d'Or is less crowded. The Canadian Abbot comes to assess the office*

---

144. We do not know who this antique dealer was.
145. Périais: we do not know who this person was.

interpreters, there is a test tomorrow. We come back by lorry. French lesson to the young cap[tain]. Visit from the French cap[-tain] who is looking for a room. 6 pm dinner with 2 Majors and the cap[tain]. (Handwritten version.)

> There had to be a Canadian, fluent in both French and English, to judge the skills of the interpreters, including 'the big ruddy-faced moron, who speaks English like Tristan Bernard's interpreter' introduced on July 19th.

Conversation until 10 in the evening with a British officer who has come to the Centre expressly to find out what seeds we lack. He will have them brought from England.

Very well versed in horticultural science, he has come from Caen for this very purpose. (Machine-typed version.)

> These few lines show how, at the time, the Garden Centre was recognised as a training school which grew products renowned in the region. The German occupation has limited them, hence the necessity to get hold of seeds.

Free at 10:30 pm but I went to bed soon after. Bad weather, rain, little sleep but little noise. Cannon fire in the distance. (Handwritten version.)

Friday, July 21st

Bad weather, raining. Floods of water in the road at Bayeux, I arrive at the office soaked. I dry myself as best I can in the kitchen and get back to work. I go to the theatre at Bayeux with a Russian girl. She is a dancer at the Opera who has walked here from Paris, in flight from the Gestapo. She found herself in Caen during the siege. When I ask her about the terror of the bombardments, she answered with Slavic calm: 'Yes, it was very noisy'. She would like to find work. We go into the little old theatre which smells of dust and dead mice and seems completely empty. In the end we find an Englishman who tells us that shows come from England all ready

The Bayeux theatre

Opened in 1830, the Bayeux theatre is located in the town centre, on rue Genas-Duhomme. Early on it was successful and hosted plays by touring companies until the arrival of cinema at the turn of the century. In the 1930s, the building fell into disuse and nearly stopped functioning. Requisitioned by the British after June 17th 1944, they were the ones programming plays, intended for the soldiers as well as the civilians. After having suffered greatly and facing unsuccessful rehabilitations, the theatre was turned into a cinema. When it was reopened in 1983, it was renamed Le Molière. It is now Le Méliès.

(Background research by Ninon Legendre.)

for performance. I invite my Russian friend to lunch at the Lion d'Or and we talk about Paris.

The Canadian abbot is back. I ask him if I could be assigned as an interpreter in Caen's agricultural department. Hitchhike home. (Handwritten version.)

The results of the language exam organised by the Canadian abbot are unknown, but Marcelle Fauchier Delavigne's request to be assigned to the agricultural department shows her implication in the management of the Garden Centre, as well as her great willingness to search for development possibilities.

When I get home, I go to sleep during the French lesson. Clearly, I cannot go on. I shall have a days' rest tomorrow.

A day like the others comes to an end …

Badges

The badges or insignias which Marcelle Fauchier Delavigne admired so much are likely those, on the one hand, of the 21st Army Group, a formation in command of the British and Canadian Troops, and on the other hand of the British Second Army, commanded by General Dempsey.

21st Army Group (two swords on a cross): this military formation gathered soldiers from the British and Canadian forces, and commanded the British Second Army and the First Canadian Army.

British Second Army (a single sword on a cross): commanded by Lieutenant General Dempsey, it served under the 21st Army Group. Two of its formations, the 1st and 30th British Corps, participated in the D-Day Landings.

Saturday, July 22nd

I have time today to pick some flowers and go round the gardens.

I rest a little. I have time to clean myself. (Handwritten version.)

Conversation with a motor-cyclist who tells me that Mr Churchill went through Saint-Gabriel last night! …

> This visit from British Prime Minister Churchill in Saint-Gabriel follows the others previously mentioned.

General Montgomery's cook comes this morning to get some vegetables and we give him flowers for the general. His men have a badge on their sleeves with two crossed swords over a cross. All the soldiers have a badge on their sleeves with a cross, but the finest of the badges is the one with a single sword right over the cross.

> General Montgomery's cook coming to pick up vegetables confirms the school's horticultural reputation.

Poor weather but no rain. The dust is now turned into such frightful mud that it is said to be holding up operations. People are talking a lot about the plot against Hitler and about revolt in Germany. Very noisy night. Little sleep.   .

Sunday, July 23rd

There is nothing in the edited version, but the pencil version presents information repeated in the blue version and the machine-typed version.

Relatively calm Sunday. In the evening, while I'm chatting with Mme Marze in the yard in front of the Centre, we see the colonel from the Intelligent [sic] Service getting out of a car accompanied by the short waiter from the Lion d'Or. To our surprise, he is staying in the room in the tower. He is tall, slim, very elegant, with a graceful walk and feet gloved in suede. He looks simultaneously friendly and snobbish. Just a few days ago Mme Marze had shared certain suspicions, could she be right?... 'This young man does not know his way in the Priory, I will guide him', he says while passing us, and walks right up to his room with him! Mme Marze looks at me, we are both dismayed. (Machine-typed version.)

Assassination attempt against Hitler

Under the codename "Operation Walkyrie", an attempt to overthrow the regime and to assassinate the Führer was made on July 20th in East Prussia, in his Rastenburg headquarters also known as 'the Wolf's Lair'. That day, a 'conspirator' successfully placed two bombs in the room where Hitler was holding a meeting; but only one of them exploded, leaving Hitler with minor injuries. This attempt was followed by severe repression by the Third Reich.

We can understand why Marcelle Fauchier Delavigne, at a time when homosexuality was considered shameful, chooses to delete this event from the edited version.

At 7 am, M. Robiquet arrived, very amiable. I hope that he will help get my car issues sorted... With M. Fox. (Handwritten version.)

Tonight, the RASC colonel invited to dinner two staff officers, working for General Eisenhower, and who came from England for inspection purposes. Very enjoyable dinner. They are all quite charming. One of them is American. Blanche's cooking is very popular. (Machine-typed version.)

I am bothered by the fact that he cannot also see his flag at the window, but it is impossible to find an American flag. (Blue version.)

A photo showing a student on top of the Tower of Justice[146] does include an American flag, implying that Marcelle Fauchier Delavigne did successfully find one at some point, at a date which is not mentioned anywhere.

I think my English skills are improving. The col[onel] notices the kitchen in the chapel and will take care of it. (Handwritten version.)

The references to the kitchen's installation in the chapel have only just begun.

Monday, July 24th

No information was kept in the final version.

Bad weather, a lot of fog. I will go back to Bayeux this morning in the pioneer's car with M. Sorel. Nothing to do at the Off[ice]. I take off to go back to Caen. I bring the little Russian dancer to have lunch with me at the Lion d'Or and then to the theatre. I can smell a little bit of the Parisian air. (Handwritten version.)

---

146. See page 154.

The little Russian dancer and I walk around Bayeux, she feels very out of place here. She is slender, pretty, blonde! She looks like a buttercup flower that has fallen into pea soup! ... (Machine-typed version.)

What to think of this metaphorical 'buttercup flower that has fallen into pea soup' which curiously follows 'slender, pretty, blonde'? It might be that, during her review, Marcelle Fauchier Delavigne was not satisfied with this metaphor and took it out ...

I come back in jip [sic] with a strange fellow, who sings and speaks with a Cockney accent. Apparently, a 'Free France' regiment has arrived in Caen to fight. Conversation with a soldier. Very nice weather, planes in [unreadable].

M. Fox arrives at 8 pm. I go for a ride with him in the car. It breaks my heart to see the old car parked under the arch like it used to be! Those were the good old days! 'Bébert'[147] seems to understand that I'm feeling emotional. So many memories!... Life... Life ended four years ago on the day I knew it had ended for Jean. Noisy night, I think, but I sleep nonetheless. (Handwritten version.)

Having her car returned is the turning point of one of the few nostalgic moments in which Marcelle Fauchier Delavigne opens up for a few words, a moment which is not kept in later versions out of modesty. Her old life, the life that ended when her son passed.

At the Centre, there is now an underlying state of war with the entire "Intelligent [sic] service'. It is serious! They have installed their kitchen in the chapel, which has greatly shocked my guest, who is becoming more and more caring for us and the Centre. I will have to stay in St Gabriel... Very nice weather tonight. Lots of planes. (Blue version.)

---

147. Bébert is Gavet's nickname.

This paragraph, not very explicit in the blue version, is a lot clearer thanks to the machine-typed version which only mentioned this event:

There is now a silent war between the Centre and the 'Intelligent [sic] Service'. The group has installed their kitchen in the chapel. Meat is being minced on a tomb: this horrifies my RASC colonel, he wants me to speak up against it. (Machine-typed version.)

This 'tomb' is the prior's tomb effigy! We are just as horrified as the Colonel was!

Tuesday, July 25th

Morning spent resting. Nice weather. A bit of exercise in the field. A little sunshine, it is nice outside. The 'water point' installation traces a path in the grass[148] *! Sad. This morning, I see M. Fox again: he knows everything ab[ou]t my car. (Handwritten version.)*

For the first time, Marcelle Fauchier Delavigne expresses regrets, after the fall of the pasture wall, because it was the pastures themselves that were transformed due to the installation of the water point, which only partially solved the dust problem. A little weariness can be felt after the euphoria of the liberation of France with the combination of noise, dust and lack of sleep.

But the col[onel] is present at break[fast] and speaks about the chapel. L[un]ch alone. What a relief! Very upset about what the pampered officers are doing in Bayeux, and about this horrendous colonel, who is good friends with all of the French Officers, likes to pee from the upstairs windows and runs after the boys. I stay in my room with my books. Only thing to do is wait... I have to go talk to the disgusting colonel who cooks in the chapel. He lets me in... And wants to hear nothing about it. I will tell my colonel about it tonight. They have damaged the tombstone, and cider has spilled

---

148. See system presentation on July 5th, page 82.

106

through the tarp on the side porch. What a group of absolute pigs! (Handwritten version.)

The colonel, our colonel, from the RASC, told me to start on a report with the help of Colonel Anderson to make him move his kitchen elsewhere! He does not know about… The rest. Complete fail, as expected. Anderson replied, 'Where do you expect me to put it?' All British Army units have installed their kitchens outside. For this purpose, they have very organised paraffin oil heaters, but I'm not brave enough to tell him. New scandal, word goes around that, last night, Anderson peed from his window! The car was unfortunately parked directly in front of the kitchen, and the trickle was very noisy … I think it might have been heard even by the highest-ranking officials! (Blue version.)

For this episode, absent from the final version, we have the testimony of the pencil version and of the blue-ink version. Marcelle Fauchier Delavigne could not bring herself to make room for this despicable behaviour, especially since she only had a limited number of pages… She is understandably upset (and who wouldn't be?), because of this reckless unit, so different from the other British soldiers!

Flowers for Montgommery [sic]. Visit from the soldier who knows Mme de Druval[149] ! Arrival of a lorry full of French soldiers. The first one kisses Mme Marze. They have dinner (why at the police station?) and leave. Distribution of Crosses of Lorraine – by a colonel. The students are delighted. I wore it proudly when it was forbidden but now… It is worn so inappropriately! (Handwritten version.)

Days go by and the new patriotic surge hurts Marcelle Fauchier Delavigne. The Cross of Lorraine, which to her symbolises the struggle for freedom, is getting so popular that it seems to lose all its meaning.

---

149. Mme de Druval is the owner of the Château de Creullet in Creully-sur-Seulles. Montgomery installed his headquarters there.

The walls are shaking. From my window I can see only part of the enormous tanks that stream along the road this morning, but over the wall I can see the top half of leather-helmeted soldiers following along, each with a radio receiver. The tall aerials tremble on the bumps. The din is deafening.

This evening a lorry arrives full of French soldiers. The first to get off sees Madame Marze and falls into her arms. They seem so happy to be with us. Some of them are said to have seized a handful of French earth as they came ashore and kissed it! ...

M. Fox arrived at 9 am t[o] pick up the car. We go to the gendarmes to take back our typewriter with the three boys. The col[onel] invited them to his room to drink whisky. He goes to pick them up at La Bonbonnière[150] ! (Handwritten version.)

> This is the moment we find out that, among all the objects confiscated by the German army, there was a typewriter. Was it the property of the school or Marcelle Fauchier Delavigne's personal typewriter? We are unaware as to whether she typed her manuscript herself or asked for the help of a secretary.

A huge explosion wakes us up in the night. I think the house is going to fall down. Windows broken.

That's all. (Machine-typed version.)

> With these very few words Marcelle Fauchier Delavigne ends her report of this day, of which she only kept military details, which is understandable: battle tanks in front of her house, return of the first French soldiers, the rest was less deserving of going down in history!

---

150. 'La Bonbonnière' (litt. The Candy Box) is the name of the instructors' place of residence, located on rue du Prieuré on the way to the castle.

Wednesday, July 26th

This morning, the weather is nice and warm. Southerly winds. A stroll with Pat in the pastures. A motor-cyclist brings Durot news from his family. Nobody left in the pine forest. Lots of departures. They create a makeshift bridge in the canal. Lun[ch] alone with the colonel. I cycle to the pastures. Some potatoes have been stolen but not as many as I thought. I get a message from Val[entine][151]: *my name and hers in her handwriting... Very moving. M. Fox arrives with my car. Very calm night. (Pencil version.)*

These few lines will later become:

The neighbourhood around the roads is impossible to live in because of the dust, but the hedges lining the pastures being open, one can go from one to the other. The pine forest where not so long ago so many soldiers were camped is now desert. The only memories left are holes in the ground filled with empty tins.

And then:

Nice sunny weather with southerly winds. This evening, I get the first message coming from the outside, a note in my sister's handwriting with both of our names on it. That's it. It means so much. (Machine-typed version.)

> Before disappearing in the final version, which allows us a glimpse at the way this woman of letters transforms on-the-spot notetaking into a print-worthy version. Her sister, Valentine Fauchier Magnan, briefly appears, marking the first contact with a person outside of the combat zone of Saint-Gabriel.

---

151. Val = Valentine, her older sister, married to Adrien Fauchier Magnan, who is Emmanuel Fauchier Delavigne's older brother: the two sisters married two brothers! She lives in Paris.

I have lunch alone today. The colonel's orderly, who waits on me, brings me the news. The English have retreated a little south of Caen. A long day. In the evening the colonel and Major Chapman seem rather thoughtful. With their same charming courtesy they offer me the traditional whisky: 'Just a very little.' But they are less cheerful than in the first days.

Marcelle Fauchier Delavigne kept a few of those reports: from July 14th to 21st and from August 23rd!

Left for Bayeux with Frederic. A motor-cyclist breaks his leg in front of the porch. In Bayeux, a little shopping. Illustrated news-papers at Deslandes'[152]. I finally have G[ener]al de Gaulle's appeal! At M. Leroy's[153] to warn him about the kitchen in the chapel. We drive by Coulon[154] on the way back, lots of detours. They ask to see my identification papers. (Handwritten version.)

The other versions go into more details about the injured motor-cyclist:

The pioneer colonel's car is driven to the ambulance on the road to Creully before taking me to Bayeux. I finally find the appeal made by G[ener]al de Gaulle on July 16th, 1940 on the back of an illustrated newspaper cover. I had begged each and every French officer, even the s[ub]-prefecture, for this declaration, but their unwillingness is evident, they feel threatened by my enthusiasm.

I nail General de Gaulle's appeal on our door. (Machine-typed version.)

As always, her patriotic enthusiasm is obvious, even though she knows it is not shared by everyone around her.

I have to visit the tax collector, he has promised me a room to house M. Robiquet's protégé; his secretary, who lives at the centre, hears the whole conversation. (Handwritten version.)

---

152. Deslandes: This person is unknown.
153. Leroy: This person is also unknown, but he could be linked to the chapel, which is a state property.
154. Coulon: actually written Coulombs, small village 3 km north of Saint-Gabriel.

Once again, a whole day which was deleted from the final version.

Weather still nice but changing. They say that progress is being made everywhere except around Caen. The people around here are afraid and complain a lot. The refugees are in awful shape, dirty and famished. One of them, a dark Indian-looking guy, stole my walking stick; when Bernard saw him in our hall two days ago and questioned him, he responded with: 'By any chance, would you have my map of Europe?' (Blue version.)

In her notes, Marcelle Fauchier Delavigne writes:

Our sports ground[155] has become a disgusting slum full of refugees. (Handwritten version.)

Long day. Tonight, I learn that the intersection on the road from La Délivrande[156] to Banville is named 'Piccadilly Circus'. Reminiscent of London... Very noisy night. (Blue version.)

Reading Mrs Dalloway[157] *takes me back to the old times! I wanted to give Lieut[enant] Lefort a letter for Colette, but he did not bother to take it. Dinner with the col[olnel] and Major Chapmann [sic]. (Handwritten version.)*

The letter is for her daughter Colette, the wife of Bernard de Menthon, who was a French Ambassador in Bern at the time: she has not seen her, or their four boys, since 1940. On July 28th, only routine information is deemed valuable: the weather, the nighttime battles. To escape this dull day, she evades through reading.

---

155. At the time, the sports ground was located outside of the priory, see map of the priory on page 144.
156. Douvres-la-Délivrande, 16 km east from Saint Gabriel.
157. Novel by Virginia Woolf, a copy is still in her house.

NAAFI (Navy, Army, and Air Force Institutes)

NAAFI was an organisation created in 1920, who supplied the British armed forces in consumer goods. This army shop provided tobacco, canned goods... And they served tea.

Saturday, July 29th

Constantly coming and going in Bayeux and nearby to interpret.

Mme Marze is disgruntled about not being allowed to go to Bayeux, she does not have an authorisation. Indeed, I have been stopped at a police roadblock and had been asked to show my identification papers. In Bayeux, fruitless search for the wine. Meeting with the American journalist. Wonderful coffee-talk with her. I stop by the office and meet Leg[158], then by NAAFI and St Sulpice[159] (nice farmers who make cider and calvados). (Handwritten version.)

> This female American journalist might be Lee Miller, one of those who were war correspondents for the US forces since 1942, and who came to Normandy mid-June 1944. Before the war, she was a model. Marcelle Fauchier Delavigne was able to identify her from magazine pictures. Nothing is known about their conversation, but the mention of a 'wonderful coffee talk' indicates that the two women got on well that day.
>
> With this episode, we also learn that Marcelle Fauchier Delavigne had been benefiting from a special treatment since the beginning, allowing her to move around freely, a privilege which was not authorized to Mme Marze.

Impossible roads, infernal noise. I am crushed with exhaustion. Getting home I take refuge at the bottom of the pasture; the dust

---

158. This person is unknown.
159. The farm is located in the Saint-Sulpice hamlet, in the village of Saint-Vigor-le-Grand, 10 km west of Saint-Gabriel.

The B-14 aerodrome in Banville

This airport, known as the B-14, was actually located on the municipalities of Amblie and Colombiers-sur-Seulles, near a large field hospital, east of the airfield. Its construction began on June 30th, and it opened on July 7th. It had a 4000 feet-long (or 1,200 meter-long) dirt landing strip. It was the only British airfield built specifically for the evacuation of seriously injured patients: 8,274 of them were flown back to England aboard those 'Dakotas', the cabins of which had been adapted to be able to carry eight stretchers. Those planes also flew celebrities, journalists and many other people who regularly travelled to and from England.[160]

reaches as far as that. The traffic in the village is such that there is a jam of tanks in front of the porch!

I don't know where to settle. I have a bad headache. But in the evening the colonel invites me come to tea tomorrow at the airfield at Banville to see the Dakotas landing. I am to go along a route worked out by him to get to the airfield; my tiredness vanishes.

I will cycle there; he shows me the way (Machine-typed version.)

In bed. I can feel a head cold coming. (Handwritten version.)

> This is the only mention of a health issue, the only sign of weakness shown by this woman, whose energy amazes us throughout the journal.

Sunday, July 30th

What surprises along the way! Everything is changed. On the road to La Délivrande, where it crosses the Courseulles road, a great

---

160. Extract from *The Administrative History of 21 Army Group on the Continent of Europe. 6 June 1944 - 8 May 1945*, Document Restricted, Nov. 1945.

crossing has been made, with a mound in the middle and an Eros on top. It is 'Piccadilly Circus'! An evocation of London... A little further, there is a graveyard of cars and other vehicles, a vast space covered with scrap-iron of the most extraordinary shapes. Finally the airfield.

In a tent the colonel and his officers offer me tea out of great brown army mugs. Then at 5 the first Dakota[161] lands. We hear it hum, it turns, descends, and parks on the ground guided by the signals of a man who looks tiny in front of such enormous obedient wings. Four other Dakotas do the same. I go up inside one of these great beasts. The openings in their sides would bleed like the men on stretchers (*gisants*) who are gradually loaded on.

Head cold, mediocre weather, as always. A few drops of rain. Mass at 9am. The weather is getting better. Despite my cold, I still go. Piccadilly Circus, road rather passable. I arrive without too much trouble. The view is splendid. (Handwritten version.)

> On this day, Marcelle Fauchier Delavigne describes the airfield and the road that leads to it, leaving out the colonel drinking whisky with the students, the weather and her cold...

M. Fox, who now uses my car, often comes to visit us; he struggles in Caen, in the middle of an inextricable mess. What a terrible waste. My enthusiasm and joy are already withering away... (Blue version.)

Monday, July 31st

Day started out cloudy, but got sunnier. Dizzy because of the head cold. Long hours.

The Intelligence [sic] Service is going to leave the chapel, the Padre complained, but where were they going to house them? They want to see me tomorrow morning. The col[onel] convinced Berrier to

---

161. See page 153.

enlist without telling anyone[162]. *Mme Marze is furious. My col[o-nel] is so sweet. He wants me to drink whisky to help with my cold. Drastic results. Very good night. (Handwritten version.)*

> Nothing was kept from these notes in the final version, neither the reference to the departure from the chapel kitchen, even though a solution still needed to be found, or the medicinal virtues of the whisky!

Tuesday, August 1st

Beautiful weather, the Americans have reached Avranches[163].

We look for a better-suited place for the I.S. [Intelligence Service] kitchen, nothing has been decided yet, maybe some part of the dining hall... Life has become unbearably obnoxious around here. A hostile feeling lingers. Almost all of the refugees have left, an American officer came to take them away... Only my two Englishmen stay every night, we have dinner together. A French officer, clean as a whistle, arrived by plane earlier today. They have a laugh about it. Noisier night. (Handwritten version.)

> These details were not deemed important enough for the final version, even though the refugees have left for an unknown destination.

Wednesday, August 2nd

> No information was kept from this day, nothing except from the fact that Marcelle Fauchier Delavigne likes to practice walking and working out: a healthy mind in a healthy body.

In the morning, headache. I force myself to do some physical activity, I also go a l[on]g walk in the f[iel]ds, and then distribution

---

162. It is unknown if the student was old enough to make this decision by himself.
163. At the end of Operation Cobra, launched on July 24th by the First US Army, Avranches, the getaway to Brittany, was freed on July 31st.

of clothes to the poor Sorel family. They are doing better. The I.S. [Intelligence Service] has not yet decided what to do with their kitchen... Great progress, it is said that Rennes and Vire have been freed[164]. Relentless gun fire all night long. (Handwritten version.)

Thursday, August 3rd

This morning, alone in the church: Mass for Jean. However, it is no longer the unity of thought, the purity of purpose. Too many preoccupations distract me. I can't pray. I have learnt that the troublesome colonel spent the night at the 'bonbonniere' (where two of our instructors live) and he said, 'Why wouldn't I sleep in Berrier's bed?' (Machine-typed version.)

The machine-typed version alone sums up the written version and the blue version. The troublesome colonel is understandably the reason for her preoccupations during Mass!

Friday, August 4th

A quiet night. I go to the s[ub-]prefecture offices to fetch a paper authorising me to pick up wood in Tracy. There is nothing to be done! A thousand people (refugees) are impatiently queuing at the front door. An hour and a half wait in the hall. I have had enough of the s[ub]prefecture. (Written version.)

The pencil notes are repeated in the machine-typed version before being removed in the final version.

At the subprefecture... impossible to go inside. I wait in vain for hours in a crowd full of poor refugees who tell me of their troubles... while some very smart ladies wearing a uniform pass us by... Too bad... I give up. (Machine-typed version).

---

164. *Rennes was freed on* August 4th, Vire on August 8th. Once more, rumours precede but predict true events.

A moving encounter today in Bayeux. A black-bereted *tankiste* (we have picked up the habit of calling them that) asks me the way: he is charming, with blue eyes like a girl's and a fair moustache like those of past times. Many of the English no longer cut off their moustaches. He has not left either his tank or the Caen area since 6 June... In the inferno of those two months! And yet today, with a gentle smile, he asks me to come and have coffee at the Lion d'Or; he is enchanted to find someone who is not in the army and can speak English. He comes to see me again at Saint-Gabriel at 7 p.m., bringing a supply of chocolate for the students and tells me that he will come back tomorrow if he is not recalled to the front. I never saw him again.

Saturday, August 5th

Very foggy in the morning. Exercising Pat in the pasture, I see tanks back there, big tanks with a sort of roller in front to detect mines. I take some flowers home. English soldiers are repairing the road: they each ask for a carnation and stick them on their berets. 'A red one for the Russians', they tell me.

[...] their fragrance reminds me of Villers[165]. (Blue version.)

> We must not forget that Russia was France's ally against Nazism at the time.

A beautiful mild evening, dinner with my friends. A peaceful night. The news is splendid: the whole of Brittany is liberated, except the big ports[166].

---

165. Villers-sur-Mer: when she was young, Marcelle Fauchier Delavigne spent her holidays at *La villa Marguerite*, owned by her mother, Emma Delavigne.
166. Although Rennes was liberated on August 4th, the American progression along the coast took longer. Vannes was liberated between 4th and 6th August, Quimper on August 8th, Saint-Malo on 17th August and Brest on 19th September. In Lorient, the German troops only surrendered on 10th May 1945!

Sunday, August 6th

Fine, with mist, in the morning.

Oh, how I would like to see someone I love! Mano, Colette. (Written version.)

After mass I go to see an English grave towards Villiers, all alone beside the little snail road. On the sleeve of his battledress, it says 'Reconnaissance.' Like Jean, he was one of the first to advance into dangerous territory... I shall take him roses. Rest all day in the sun beside the window[167], reading a little.

Then on the sofa of my bedroom. In the evening, dinner with five English of the g[eneral] s[taff]. I am very interested in a Communist English soldier. Quiet night; sleepy. (Machine-typed version.)

A good evening with the English.

> Marcelle Fauchier Delavigne seems to have been in great need of rest. This need primarily manifests through her reading activities. The wide windowsill in her bedroom, opening out onto the courtyard, enables her to sit comfortably, away from prying eyes, under the mild sun of this summer day.

Monday, August 7th

Heavy fog. It will be a fine day. I bring some roses to the English grave on the Villiers coast. Pat, nasty, refuses to follow me. On my way back, I meet Blanche, a linen seller, who comes to pick me up. Two officers are in the office to deal with the 'nancy boy' Colonel. The whole morning is devoted to the report that will be signed by M. Marze, and the whole afternoon, until 7 p.m. to the one signed by Bernard. It is only at 8:30 p.m. that I am ready to go downstairs and drink whisky with five officers who are dining. Quiet night, but stuck indoors the whole day, I don't sleep well. (Machine-typed version).

---

167. See page 160.

These notes written in the evening become, in the blue version:

The whole day is spent with two officers from General Montgomery's general staff who come to do an investigation on Colonel Anderson. Our RASC general staff had got wind of what was going on at the Center and notified the higher ranks of it. Major Chapman in particular is a true friend to us. I am wrong to only speak about Major Chapman, they are all perfect friends.

Before the machine-typed version:

Because of the suspicious behaviour of the colonel from the 'Intelligent [sic] service' that has drawn the attention of Colonel Kraig, who is staying at my place, an investigation has been initiated and two officers from General Montgomery's general staff are coming to question us. The situation is a little awkward and sometimes rather funny. How can I speak in English about things I am not used to describing in French without a little embarrassment.

This unpleasant episode for Marcelle Fauchier Delavigne completely disappears in the final version!

Tuesday, August 8th

Weather still cold and foggy. It will be sunny later today. I am called to the Centre to speak to the gendarme to make a deposition against X[168]... which I sign, then arrival of the 2 Englishmen from yesterday, deposition against the col[onel] which I also sign and then l[un]ch. After lunch Ladreit, Gavet and Durot are questioned, m[illegible]... I have a chat with Mme Marze, with a British navy officer and with a French soldier. In the evening, 2 handsome French paratroopers. They have dinner at the Centre. The students have been restless since the investigation. I am introduced to the new chief col[onel]. Quiet night but not enough physical exercise to sleep well. (Handwritten version.)

This day was not kept in the blue version and is completely erased.

---

168. X. is one of the villagers accused of collaboration.

Sunny weather as usual. Slight N-E wind. The paratroopers are back, and they are investigating X. They ask me to testify under oath that he collaborated with the enemy. It is a bit intimidating.

Later on, Bernard asks for my help with a cap[tain] freshly arrived from Algeria. Very interesting. Giraud is just like I thought he would be, 'L'armée d'Alger, pourri' [sic][169] ! … But de Gaulle, a 'superhuman'. It's his turn of phrase. He asks about F. de Menthon[170] and about Jean the first[171]. I search with him for a place for a bakery (quick stop by Marie Charlot's)[172].

An old and tall RAF soldier also visits, he is half-French and very pleasant. He says he will stop by again. He looks a bit like an older Bernstein[173]. A lot of others that have come to get vegetables.

I put some flowers back into the house. Poor dusty begonias! War is declared with the satyr col[onel]. He walks in front of me without greeting me. Well, that's that. Mme Marze tells me that while the officers were having tea, he spent 45 minutes chatting with Berrier[174]. The nights have become completely calm. (Handwritten version.)

A French captain coming from Alger. He harshly criticises the Army of Africa formed by the Vichy regime: "They are not soldiers; they are bad government workers."

Lots of others come to pick up vegetables. The Centre yard is constantly full of lorries coming in and out. (Blue version.)

---

169. Translation: 'Algerian army, all rotten!'
170. François de Menthon is Colette's step-brother (she is married to Bernard de Menthon). This family connection earned her visits from the Germans investigating him.
171. It is not clear as to whether he is speaking of Jean I or about Jean (her son) first of all…
172. See note on page 46.
173. Henri Bernstein (1876-1953), French playwright; he led the Théâtre du Gymnase in Paris, and later the café-théâtre Les Ambassadeurs.
174. Berrier: it seems he had not enrolled yet!

General Henri Giraud (1879-1949)

Stationed in Alger after November 1942, this military chief was first assigned to the civil and military command of French North Africa. He received support from the Allied Forces, particularly from the US, towards the rearmament of the Army of Africa. In June 1943, alongside General de Gaulle, he was appointed co-chairman of the French Committee of National Liberation (*Comité français de Libération nationale*, or CFLN). Soon after, disagreements grew between the two men: de Gaulle wanted to cut any remaining ties with Vichy France, to which Giraud remained more or less linked. Then, the former criticised the latter on his decision to lead the liberation of Corsica by himself in the autumn of 1943. Forced to leave his role in the CFNL, Giraud was demoted to the symbolic function of Inspector General of the Army. Until late September 1944, he lived in a confiscated property in Mazagran, where he was simultaneously protected and monitored by the French forces. After the liberation of France, he was elected deputy of Moselle and member of the Constituent Assembly of the French Fourth Republic.

Nothing was kept from that day in the final version, even though Marcelle Fauchier Delavigne's conscience of the importance of her signing the testimony against the collaborating villager is shown: "It is a bit intimidating".

Then her enthusiasm for de Gaulle returns, with the confirmation that, in spite of the events, the Garden Centre keeps its activity: people come to buy vegetables.

François de Menthon

François de Menthon was a French legal expert, born in the Jura region. He enlisted in the army in 1939. He was captured during the 'Phoney War', successfully escaped and joined the Resistance. Close to Jean Moulin, he was one of the leaders of the Combat movement. In 1943, he joined de Gaulle in London and later in Algiers, where he became commissioner of justice in the CFLN.

After the liberation of France, François de Menthon was named minister of justice in de Gaulle's government, and lead prosecutor at the Nuremberg War Crimes Tribunal.

Thursday, August 10th

Pat is ill. He can only drag himself around. He has eaten too much English canned food.

These cans are labelled 'Porcs [sic] and vegetables', mysterious string of words that Blanche translates to 'Vegetarian pork' which can only mean incredibly dangerous food, at least in her opinion! (Machine-typed version.)

I go to Bayeux.

Cycle to see Suz[anne][175] as far as Esquay by taking the narrow path[176]. (Handwritten version.)

Beautiful warming sun.

I have asked for a permit to go to Caen. Denied, as expected. In Bayeux, nice visit to the major at the employment centre. I will bring him workers. (Handwritten version.)

The townspeople seem to be coming alive a bit. They are beginning to flourish.

---

175. Suzanne de Bourgoing.
176. A path going through farmlands that helps avoiding the road and military vehicles.

In front of Deslandes' house, Jacques Roussel[177] stops me to announce that he has enlisted and that he will join the navy in England. I congratulate him. (Blue version.)

Every evening people gather in the sports field to listen to the news. The radio is put in an apple tree. The night is noisy. Yesterday two planes were shot down.

Friday, August 11th

Beautiful warm weather. I go to bathe in the river. Three Englishmen are there doing their washing; others, half-naked, are sunbathing. I chat with them for an hour.

Today Blanche's son, Lucien, arrives. He comes from Villers-sur-Mer and has bicycled 60 kilometres, through the fronts around Avranches, carrying his bicycle across the River Mayenne. He is very proud of his achievement.

With all the bridges blown up, joining the American lines near Avranches, and giving information to the Allied troops about everything he saw. (Machine-typed version.)

I find the day oppressive. Now the Americans are advancing on Paris, wild rumours abound. Everyone tells sensational news, which is then denied next morning… When I ask my colonel about an advance, I always get the same answer: 'Maybe.' And he smiles.

The troops, according to those we meet, are 100, 80, 60 or even 50 kilometers away from Paris… They have passed Chartres, Rambouillet… I am fuming. What would they know? (Blue version.)

All of those fools are getting on my nerves, they all want to know more than their neighbour does! … (Handwritten version.)

---

177. Jacques Roussel is one of the persons managing the Saint-Gabriel flour mill.

Lahaulle[178] told me that the Germans were launching manned tor-pedoes from Villiers, to sink ships in Courseulles' harbour. He did not tell the Americans when they questioned him, because he was scared Villers would be bombed. This evening, I give the information to my colonel. (Blue version.)

No news in the field, I go and sit with everyone else in front of the Centre, Major Chapman and the linen sales lady are still sat on the garden wall at 10 pm. Very sweet. Quiet night, but I do not sleep well, very nervous. (Handwritten version.)

Days go by. Marcelle Fauchier Delavigne makes the most of the pleasant weather and goes swimming in the river, while the soldiers are resting, bathing, washing their laundry – if they have not tasked a village girl with it yet[179]. But History meddles with this relaxing day, the American progressing towards Paris and Marcelle Fauchier Delavigne becoming an informant… and sharing the testimony of Lucien Lahaulle, son of her loyal Blanche.

Saturday, August 12th

Not a line in the final version, and yet how much was there to say!

They are leaving, they are all leaving, they have left… The whole "Intelligent Service" has left this morning. Quickly, without a word, folding their tents, loading the lorries, they disappeared, much to our great pleasure.

Beautiful weather today. Autumn breeze. Poor M. Robiquet visits us, he is scrawny and looks very different. He is still sleeping in a basement…

Tonight, Miss Hood and an RAF nurse bring in a squadron leader from Courseulles. We all dine together. Blanche went above

---

178. Here, Lucien Lahaulle, one of Blanche's sons.
179. Testimony of Ted Bates, *Royal Engineers, who slept in a tent on rue du clos Saint-Benoît.*

and beyond. We share the British provisions. Nothing beats those informal dinners, this simple life shared with honest and humble people. Alas, my colonel and Major Chapman are going to leave us to go to Brécy, where they will have more room. What a shame! (Blue version.)

The Centre is finally back to normal since the I.S. has left, all the students are singing in the hall, a tank has fallen into the river, it is full of oil. Good night. (Handwritten version.)

> The chapel is cleared of its occupants, the Centre itself is coming back to life. The war is still ongoing: a tank fell in the river!

Sunday, August 13th

Very nice weather. The Centre is back to normal. I can hear the students singing in the kitchen, which means that Mme Marze is happy. Nothing to report. (Blue version.)

> These few lines were deleted from the final version.

Monday, August 14th

This morning I am fuming. A bunch of kids wearing armbands, like those of the FFI[180], broke into the bindery and turned it upside down. Why didn't they just come and ask me for a room key? They are to leave soon by lorry. (Blue version.)

They drank tea at the Centre and left by lorry. I had a chat with Berrier who wanted to leave. He stays. (Handwritten version.)

> For the first time, Marcelle Fauchier Delavigne speaks about those youngsters impersonating the FFI, wanting to prove their strength, while the infamous colonel has not yet managed to convince Berrier to enrol: he ends up staying at the Centre!

---

180. French Forces of the Interior, French Resistance.

Trip to Creully to get a bicycle permit, valid in the region and, if possible, as far as Caen. (Blue version.)

It is still difficult to move around and travel: permits are mandatory.

Impossible to bathe this morning. A tank has fallen into the river and the water is full of petrol. I go to Bayeux. Coming back I find the refugee ladies and girls from Caen with two or three English paras, and Frederick the trapezist, who, it seems clear, has found a sweetheart.

This evening, at half past seven, a squadron leader arrives from Courseulles: he calls up to me through the window. I quickly put on my new dress and jump into the jeep; we go through Banville to pick up Kay Hood and one of her colleagues, and arrive, blown away, at a little seaside villa transformed into a theatre. Good jokes, much laughter from all the audience, almost entirely made up of the RAF; marvellous atmosphere. From time to time the loud voice of guns from the sea makes the walls shake or there is the explosion of a German shell. They are still falling almost every evening on Courseulles. When we leave, the night is dark, with gusts of wind, a nice smell of seaweed, and salt on ones' lips. We grope under lowered shutters. It is the mess. A small room full of hanging lamps. Through the smoke I see a lot of grey-blue uniforms. An impression of a dream come true. Marvellous. Home by jeep. We hurtle through wind and darkness. Fireworks all around, from anti-aircraft batteries at Arromanches and Caen, and finally a salvo welcomes us at our arrival at Saint-Gabriel. I shall never forget this night.

Avalanche of shrapnel, my companions take shelter at my place while we wait for the all-clear signal. My French adjectives are not strong enough to describe the fragile, intoxicating and passionate charm of a night like this! (Machine-typed version.)

I shall never forget this night.

A night to remember!

Tuesday, August 15th

Tired of the constant din of the planes flying over us. (Handwritten version.)

Coming out from mass I am accosted by an officer who has come to engage me to act as interpreter in a camp at Ducy-Sainte-Marguerite[181]. It is joy to be able to be of service. I begin work tomorrow. Very threatening weather ending with a storm. Our English friends leave for Brécy.

I cannot sleep. Muggy weather and what is happening in Paris? (Handwritten version.)

> Despite her new activity, Marcelle Fauchier Delavigne is still worried about the lack of news from Paris, where her husband was working.

August 16th-25th

> In the final version, these days are grouped together, which is not the case in the pencil version. This results in a carefully drafted text, gathering day-to-day notes and leaving out numerous details in order to give a homogenous presentation to those days in the military camp. This shows her true writing skills!

August 16th

The RASC leaves at 8:30 am to go to Audrieu. The English insist on hiring me (with payment). (Handwritten version.)

An army car comes to collect me at half past eight every morning and brings me back at half past seven in the evening. The work is interesting. It is about the organization of a camp where all the spare parts of army vehicles, tanks, tractors etc are to be stored. it

---

181. Ducy-Sainte-Marguerite, village located on the other side of the N13, 6 km from Saint-Gabriel.

is an immense affair, covering several kilometres of land. They are making a railway line from Audrieu station.

Though even more important, it is rather the same kind of camp as the one I saw started on the road from Littry to Bayeux. On one side are tents, a lot of tents for clerical work: forms to be counted, classified, catalogued, etc. On the other side, great canvas-covered galleries for the stores and maintenance work. Everything is gradually going up while new workers, men and women, arrive every day from Caen. There must be many of them, I am told nine to ten thousand. And they are all taken on. My job is to find out where to send them. Sitting beside the major every morning, I watch this sad line of unfortunates come from the inferno of Caen. They are most of them in a pitiable state. I question them to find out the best use to be made of each of them.

I lunch in a big tent with the women workers. Cooking is done out of doors. Cars bring all the provisions: canned food, dried vegetables (carrots, cabbages, potatoes), white bread, even water is brought in lorries. The English are extremely kind to the workers, paying attention to the least complaint. I have the job of going with any of the men or women who may have need of care to a doctor from nearby, who is in a tent to which we are taken every day by car. The workers are brought from Caen and taken back in lorries.

The departure is always very cheerful. Many of the women are young, and they laugh, jump into their lorries, and go off singing loudly. On rainy days we have to cross a sea of mud to get to the maintenance area. The women assemble armaments in the galleries out of spare parts which fit together simply like children's meccano. But the work has to be supervised. One day the major wants to take me by car, the car gets stuck, and when I get out my galoshes remain stuck in the mud! ...

Since the official news has told us that the American armies are at the gates of Paris, my Parisian heart has been trembling. The workwomen bring me more alarming stories every day. 'Paris is dying of hunger. The black flag is flying over the town, which means starvation. The town is half destroyed; the monuments are blown up.' Finally on Wednesday 23 August, when for the first time the radio is turned on in the tent during breakfast, we hear: 'Paris has just been liberated by the French home forces (*les Forces Françaises de l'Intérieur*).' Shouts of applause and the radio plays the 'Marseillaise': we bellow it in chorus. Paris is liberated, but in what condition? Going back to Saint-Gabriel, I find a message from the colonel at Brécy, brought by the headquarters motor-cyclist. It is a communiqué with these words marked in red: 'Liberation of Paris by the French[182].'

The English come round all evening to congratulate us. From this moment I am no longer alive. The most contradictory rumours go around. I stamp about with impatience. How to get back to Paris, my poor, bleeding Paris? I go to Ducy for two more days, but there are now several interpreters at the camp who can replace me. I make my excuses to the major, who is charming and understanding like all his compatriots, and regain my liberty. I have heard that the day before yesterday a pilot from Vaux-sur-Seulles was offering a seat in his plane. I shall go tomorrow to find out.

> As the days pass, Marcelle Fauchier Delavigne gets increasingly worried about her husband, from whom she has not yet received any news. She grows impatient to the point of leaving her job and considering taking a plane to Paris!

> Extracts from the paper version, a few added entries:

August 16th

I am in charge of the women. They are given forms to fill in. Little by little, they get used to the task.

They sing. Their songs are quite wistful, they always make me feel sentimental and a little nostalgic. They seem very happy. The farm ones are also very nice.

---

182. See page 158: *Daily news* from August 23rd.

August 17th

I have to choose future monitors, not an easy task! Very nice weather. L[un]ch with the female workers. Very nice l[un]ch. It is such a pleasure to feel useful. At l[un]ch, and in the evening in the lorries, the workers sing En passant par la Lorraine[183]*, they are all very joyful. I have received good news about Paris. I can finally breathe a little.*

August 18th

New female workers are coming in every day. An officer tells me that a note from Colette has arrived. I don't know anything about it! Tonight, the col[onel] and the friendly major visit us, very optimistic. I dine with the pioneer col[onel], I am tired and hope to get some sleep.

August 19th

Good workday. I feel much happier and how great are the news! And then the workers call for me so nicely. But a lot of work to do. I have to be everywhere! Visit from the chief colonel. Pat is not doing good, it's very sad. I dine with the sweet Kay Hood and the officer from Courseulles. It is impossible to know anything from Colette's note.

Sunday, August 20th

The pioneers are leaving. The Centre is starting to get back to normal. I rest and clean Mano's room. I have the feeling that he will return soon. The events in Paris have me… quivering. Pat is doing better; the vet reassures us. I feel less anxious. Tonight, dinner with our friends from Brécy's H[ead].Q[uarter].

Monday, August 21st

I cannot get my hands on Colette's note. When I return, 2 visits from Major Chapman. They want to move back in. He will be here tomorrow night to discuss it.

---

183. Traditional French song,

130

Tuesday 22nd

Very good news from the fat airmen: Toulouse, Bordeaux, Grenoble, Lyon are taken. He said that Paris is too, for the most part, it is finished... So much emotions.

Wednesday 23rd

I send young Blanche to Brécy. They won't come. They sent me the news of the liberation of Paris.

Thursday 24th

60 newcomers[184]. The days are starting to be long and rough for me, as soon as I'm back home I try to find a way to go to Paris. Visit from the Col and Chapman.

Friday 25th

Very nice weather, long day in Ducy. I almost can't bear it anymore. In the morning, I visited the new installation (no 1)... I tell them I won't be coming the next day. When I'm back the D[octo]r is here. We go to the castle to see the Lahaulle boy. The D[octo]r will come back tomorrow to bandage Legris' son[185], an amputee. At 9am I'll go listen to the news and have some whiskey with the new, very nice, colonel in the bindery. I make my plans to go to Paris. M. Fox lends me his car (this is very nice of him). (Handwritten version.)

Saturday, August 26th

Fruitless journey to Vaux-sur-Seulles. The airmen have already left.

Today I can get dressed without haste again. I go up the Villiers ridge to bring some roses to the grave of the English soldier, then I have lunch with the Scottish Doctor and Miss Hood, who are here to care for the son of a refugee who had is hand amputated.

---

184. Who are these newcomers? Could they be refugees?
185. He is the son of a refugee.

Afternoon, in Bayeux on my bike. The road is much nicer now, much less traffic and dust. I waited 2 hours for someone who knew the airman. I only learn now that he left Vaux. I am too late, alas!

Pénais[186] can give me some fuel to go to Paris, but only if I take him there. I agree with M. Fox. I took my decision quickly. We will leave tomorrow. Robin[187] arrived in the evening, he said that M. Fox told him that it is impossible to enter Paris. The roads are barred 30 kilometres (19 miles) from the city!... My plans fell apart.

Robin, with the buttery voice of a wounded peasant, paints a strange picture of the capture of Caen. He was a stretcher-bearer, he e...[illegible] a Boche himself at the turn of a wall, he ran everywhere while houses collapsed, and when we ask him "Weren't you afraid?" he answers calmly: "Well, I had to see something?".
(Blue version.)

The most important part of this day is the airmen's departure, summed up in a single sentence: I am too late, alas!

Sunday, August 27th

This morning, on arriving at mass, I meet Abbé Tolmer with a newspaper in his hand. The news he gives me is terrifying: Paris no longer exists. All the monuments have been demolished. There was already talk yesterday of the destruction of the two Gabriel[188] palaces. Can it be that from the Concorde bridge one can no longer see them under the fair Paris sky? I shiver. 'Alas, Madame,' he adds, 'sixty thousands deaths are reported.' Madame Marze no longer recognizes me when I go into the church. I am apparently green. I have decided I shall go tomorrow, at whatever cost.

---

186. Unidentified person.
187. Likewise.
188. Marcelle Fauchier Delavigne refers to the two palaces lining the rue Royale: the Crillon hotel and the Coislin hotel on one side of the street and the *hôtel de la Marine* on the other, on the *place de la Concorde*.

A long sultry day threatening a storm. This evening I am invited to dinner with the staff at Brécy. Before dinner there will be a film show for the troops. Shut into this dark, airless room I feel very uncomfortable. How can I get through it? I have a struggle and emerge victorious. But it will be impossible to eat whatever there is at dinner. The young nurses surround me with attentions. Everyone overcomes me with kindness. The table is laid in one of the rooms once so well furnished by Rachel Boyer[189]. The Boches carried off all they found there, even the hangings, and left some obscene drawings on the walls as a memento of their presence. Impeccable service. The crockery, flowers, and several chairs come from Saint-Gabriel. The colonel is absolutely determined to sustain me with whisky: 'Just a very little…' I begin to feel better.

Suddenly someone comes to tell me that Blanche is asking for me, with such a funny face… I rush out, excited. Mano[190] is on the steps! and Paris is saved!

The next evening, Kay and Hill arrive along with two others from Banville, also a visit from the small half-Russian airman. (Handwritten version.)

The pencil notes end on this sentence.

The printed version of 1945-1946 adds a small word after "Mano is on the steps! and Paris is saved!"

THE END

The strain of the last 3 months ends with the arrival of her husband, the management of the garden Centre and of the contact with the English soldiers will be shared at last. The imperious necessity to write down the details of each day vanishes.

End of the episode…

---

189. Rachel Boyer (1864-1935), actress of the Comédie-Française and philanthropist. She bought the castle of Brécy in 1943.
190. See page 160.

REMEMBRANCES[191]

In homage of the memory of Madame Marcelle Fauchier Delavigne

René Fox, former head of the agricultural services of freed Calvados and Cotentin departments (1944), general engineer of agriculture (ret.)

September 1980

She went through life with a determined gait…

When I was head of the agricultural services in the Calvados department, I was tasked, in 1933, to present a conference in front of the students of the Saint-Gabriel gardening learning Centre.

I remember that I was there to talk about a newcomer in Normandy, the Colorado potato beetle, destructor of solanums and raider – before other intruders some years later - of our harvests.

After having located the Centre, lodged at the end of a tortuous village street, I discovered its porch leading to a unique sight. A large Norman courtyard populated by apple trees with knotted crowns reaching toword the sun in a beautiful summer afternoon. All around it, bathed in golden light from the sun's reflection, the courtyard was surrounded by old buildings, I could sense them bending under the weight of the centuries.

---

191. Text initially published in 1984 in the appendix of the first reedition of *Three Months with the English.*

However, expert hands seemed to have given them some new life.

The most memorable event, however, was my first meeting with two unknown characters who were now going up the alley. The first was a tall man with an elegant gait, wearing a soft hat with a carelessly raised edge, and you could easily see his qualities as an organiser. Alongside him was a smaller woman, walking with small quick steps and very simply dressed. The man seemed to be enraptured by the porch and its stones. The woman had intelligent, blinking eyes, and, her head slightly tilted, she seemed to follow a thought or vision completely alien to her environment.

She advanced with the same determined gait that I would learn to recognise.

When they saw me at last, they had a reflex that was customary for the earthlings of the time when they were before someone with a portfolio. Said portfolio contained the text for my conference. They gave me a very polite welcome.

Thus began a very long and very trusted friendship with M. and Mme Fauchier Delavigne.

The garden Centre, ever-expanding, was very satisfying and we always had a project in mind. But fate destined us to live exceptional events as well. In times such as these, you come to truly know those around you. Haven't Tacitus said that time puts one back to their just and proper place? Such was the case at the garden Centre.

In 1939 the Centre stayed open.

In 1940, we didn't understand at first... but we realized what was going on soon enough. The Centre became a constant concern. In turn, M. and Mme Fauchier Delavigne came to assist M. and Mme Marze who ensured the safety, subsistence and teaching of around forty boys.

From time to time, we could also catch a glimpse of Mme Françoise[192], always pensive, brave and quiet. She had two sons, Alain and Hervé, who took up the torch many years later.

When the danger became evident, it was decided that Madame (as the great lady of this house was called) would stay in Saint-Gabriel. You should have seen her, taking part in "top-level" meetings during which, in the secrecy of Mme Marze's bedroom, grave questions were discussed, and decision-making took place.

You also should have seen her accompanying me to the German work services in Caen that wanted to force the students to accomplish tasks not to be done by children. I lamented the fact that she imposed such strains on herself. But I think that those we talked to thought the same because, in the end, they backed down.

The Centre was the house of God. Its porch, always open, welcomed inside friends of the household, but also refugees and strangers – on Mme Fauchier Delavigne's orders. A truly Benedictine tradition. In the dining hall, which was filled with friends, the meals included Jerusalem artichokes and rutabaga garnished with pork or rabbit bred by M. Marze, a wise man. Every week, I would have a nice meal at the Centre because, as a teacher, I could have lunch there every Tuesday.

Around fifty people, students included, lived in the Centre. This is without considering several dogs, and an unknown number of cats, along with their litter, and which population obviously went up following an almost geometric progression. I never managed to reduce their numbers. I was told that the amount of pest at the time justified their high numbers – which was quite true. However, I never thought about any causality

192. Wife of Jean Fauchier Delavigne, her husband dies in 1940 and she gives birth the same year to her two sons. She remarries with Pierre de Menthon in 1945.

between the proliferation of cats and the number of menus that included rabbit stew.

The administrative and financial management of the Centre was entrusted to Mme Marze. She was a strong-willed woman, graced with a natural cunning that could confuse the most authentic Normans, or the highest-ranking occupiers. Gentle and friendly, she so seldom said no that you could think the word was unknown to her. Which did not mean that she was not listening to you. Every morning, before sunrise, she would prepare the projects of the day, alone in her office. She was a compassionate woman who taught me much.

Her husband, M. Marze, was a very good manager, very capable and experimented. He was held in high-esteem due to his past as a soldier in the Great War. His presence was reassuring.

Their son, Bernard, competent and active, overcame hardships with humour. He was friend with everyone. His students held him in high regards. We got along very well.

Mme Fauchier Delavigne liked to use a bike which – apart from its age – was unremarkable. One day however, she came toward me bicycling with a lively air, which made me think that she had heard good news from the war. But the bike seemed to be prettier than ever. Then, I saw a magnificent Cross of Lorraine[193], in full light, just above the front of the frame (where the address of the owner was written). Thus, in the middle of a restricted area, the symbol of free France travelled the country, to the horror of her friends.

Bayeux, the first liberated town, was the French capital until July 9th, 1944. The town stayed an administrative centre under the authority of our friend Triboulet[194]. Very active and competent, he was a flexible manager. In Caen, amidst the ruins,

_____

193. The Cross of Lorraine was used as a symbol of Free France during World War II and was earlier used by French patriots to signify desire to reclaim provinces lost to Germany in the Franco-Prussian War.
194. Raymond Triboulet was appointed as the first subprefect of liberated France in Bayeux on the 15th of June 1944.

the scrupulous M. Daure, prefect of the liberation, was seeing the windows of his office hit by enemy bullets. Around him, embryos of reassembled services had a branch in Bayeux. This is how the office of agricultural services of Caen came to have an annex at the Général-de-Dais Street in Bayeux. My duties thus often called me to go there, in the company of English and American officers. Notably, it was there that we held our committees – we were in France once more, weren't we? – to study the issues of the day.

The decisions, of a surprisingly international nature, often used military means. To move throughout the whole liberated zone, which was thankfully extending, I had the choice between my bike, an English Jeep or an American motorbike. As I was not a biking champion, and also to go faster in the incredible dust clouds of the convoys, I preferred to use motorized means. They were driven by soldiers, with wide leather belts around the waist. The roads were in a very bad state, wrecked by tank threads and pierced with innumerable craters, and you can guess that it was quite an ordeal to jump from one crater to another with a war machine almost devoid of any shock absorbers.

In July 1944, as I was going through Saint-Gabriel on my bike, I encountered Mme Fauchier Delavigne who complimented my long face that was not fit for a "liberated", so I told her the causes. As soon as she learned that I was in charge of the French agricultural service and that, on this basis, I was part of this long-awaited French Republic, she got her own car out and said that I could use it for as long as I liked and how I wanted.

If I mention this, it is because in the days that followed, as I was going through Bayeux to go to the American-liberated Cotentin, I saw at Saint-Patrice square Mme Fauchier Delavigne who was pushing her bike by the handles, while I was in a comfortable car which neither belonged to the state, nor to the Allies, and which also had a Parisian license plate. Undoubtedly, everyone wondered about this Renault who brought along the spirit of a still-occupied Paris.

As I was on the road in the middle of a military convoy which would not stop no matter what, I tried to make a friendly wave towards Mme Fauchier Delavigne, who did not see me and disappeared into the crowd.

So she went, always with her determined gait, towards the English office where she gave it all in order to serve.

APPENDIX

Family tree

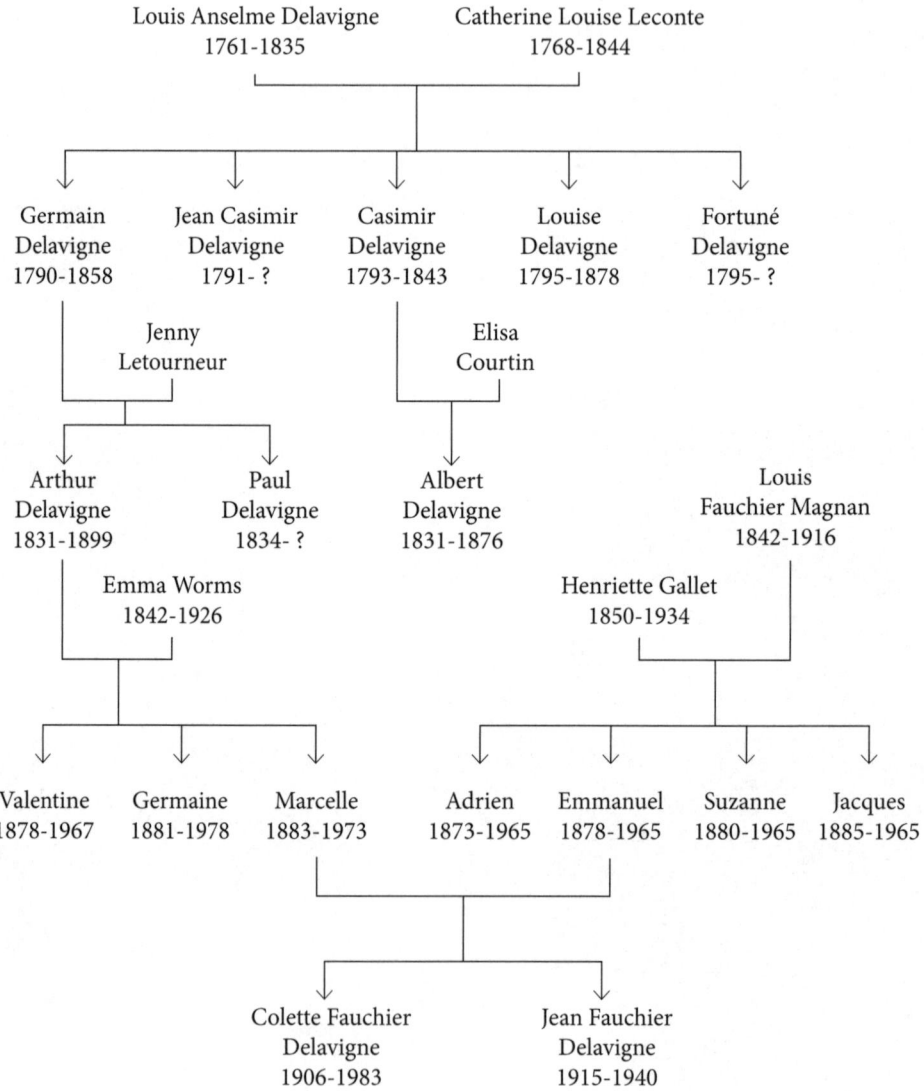

Louis Anselme Delavigne 1761-1835 — Catherine Louise Leconte 1768-1844

Germain Delavigne 1790-1858 | Jean Casimir Delavigne 1791- ? | Casimir Delavigne 1793-1843 | Louise Delavigne 1795-1878 | Fortuné Delavigne 1795- ?

Jenny Letourneur

Elisa Courtin

Arthur Delavigne 1831-1899 | Paul Delavigne 1834- ? | Albert Delavigne 1831-1876 | Louis Fauchier Magnan 1842-1916

Emma Worms 1842-1926

Henriette Gallet 1850-1934

Valentine 1878-1967 | Germaine 1881-1978 | Marcelle 1883-1973 | Adrien 1873-1965 | Emmanuel 1878-1965 | Suzanne 1880-1965 | Jacques 1885-1965

Colette Fauchier Delavigne 1906-1983 | Jean Fauchier Delavigne 1915-1940

Site plan

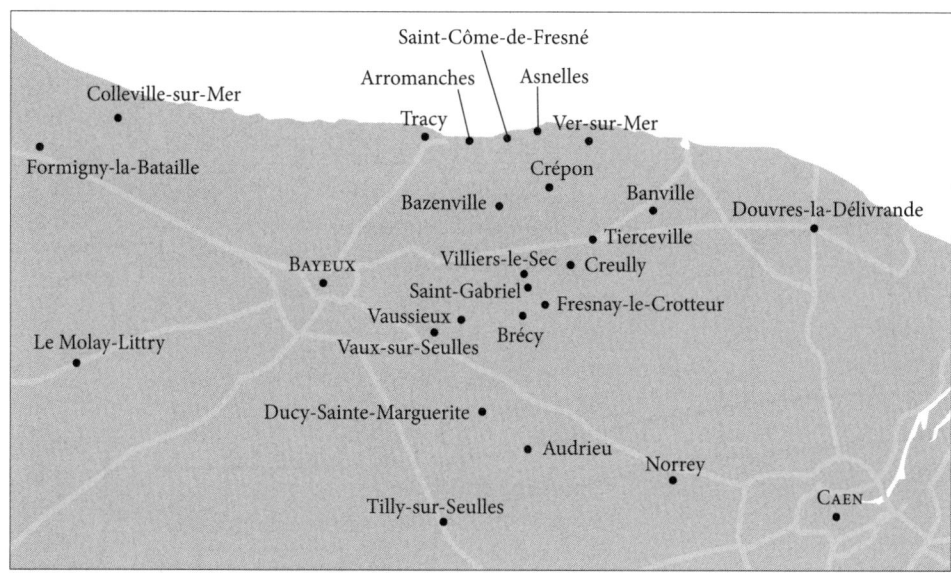

Map of Saint-Gabriel village

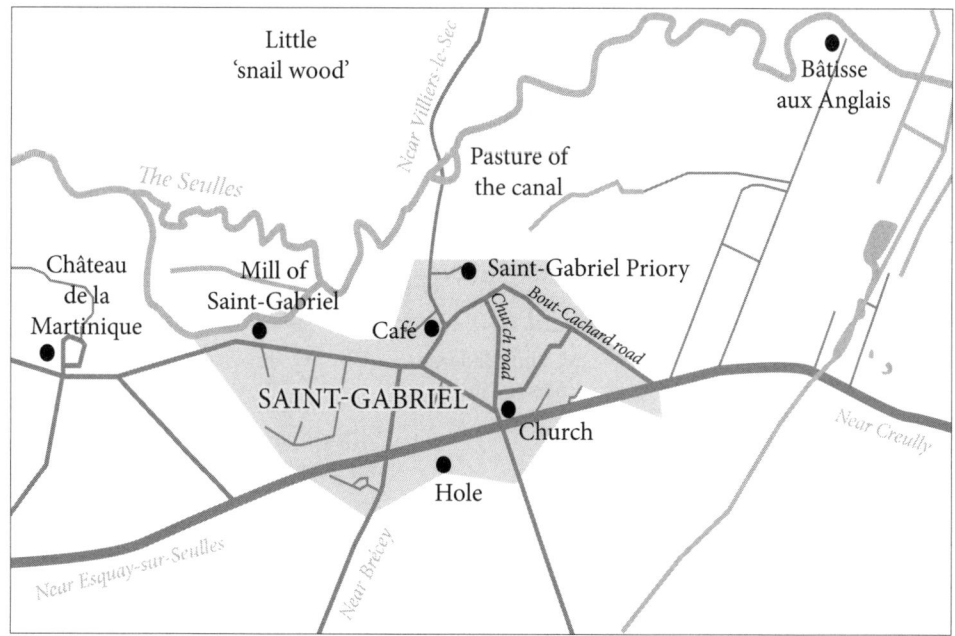

Map of Saint-Gabriel priory – ground floor

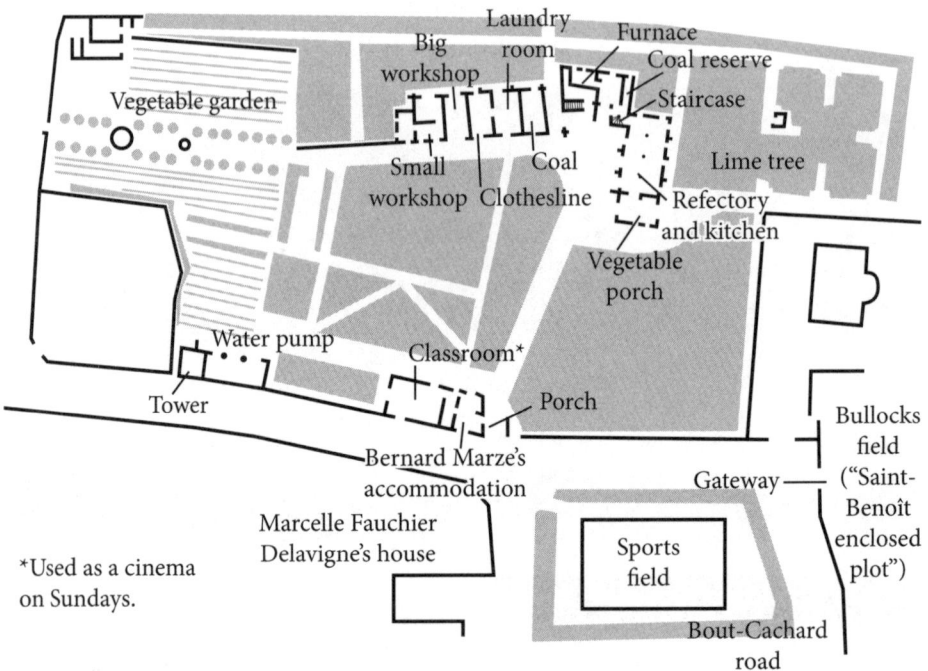

Big workshop
Laundry room
Furnace
Coal reserve
Staircase
Vegetable garden
Small workshop
Coal
Clothesline
Lime tree
Refectory and kitchen
Vegetable porch
Water pump
Classroom*
Tower
Porch
Bernard Marze's accommodation
Bullocks field ("Saint-Benoît enclosed plot")
Gateway
Marcelle Fauchier Delavigne's house
Sports field
*Used as a cinema on Sundays.
Bout-Cachard road

Marie Charlot's house

Map of Saint-Gabriel priory – first floor

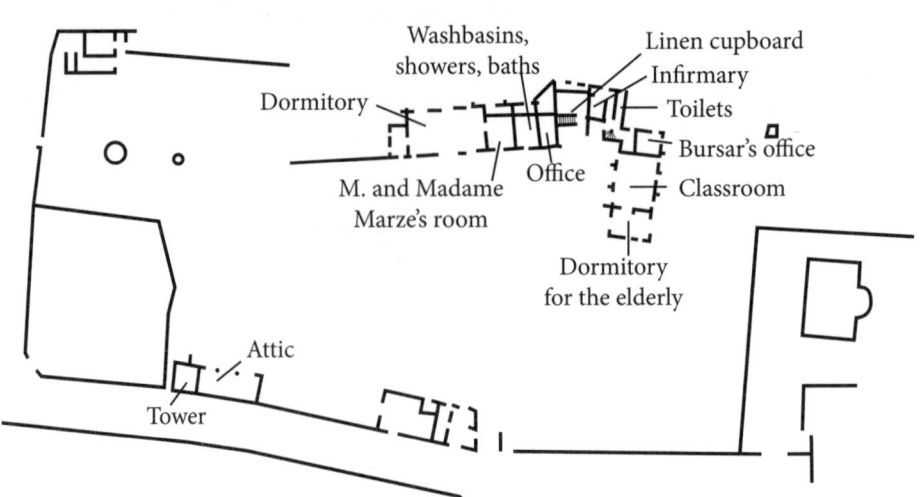

Washbasins, showers, baths
Linen cupboard
Infirmary
Dormitory
Toilets
Bursar's office
Office
M. and Madame Marze's room
Classroom
Dormitory for the elderly
Attic
Tower

de la préfecture, Robiquet, Bienfait, Sorel, sont sains et saufs, mais le directeur des Services Agricoles M. Debot est très gravement blessé et de ses enfants tués. Dîner seul avec le grand major Hodgson. Très cordial, le bon colonel. Il aime parler un français mêlé d'espagnol, et se réjouit d'aller à Paris pour passer toute la nuit à Montmartre. Vive canonnade —

Dimanche 16 juillet

Il y a maintenant une messe à 9h dite par l'abbé Tolmer, cousin des Roussel et réfugié ici. Joie de ne plus assister à cette grand messe où l'on se bat pour entrer. Temps très lourd — Je me promène avec Pat dans les herbages qui longent la rivière derrière la reculée. Le seul endroit de St Gabriel où l'herbe soit encore un peu verte. La poussière est pour nous un véritable fléau, je ne pensais pas qu'elle put atteindre ces proportions, tous les arbres, tous les toits, tous les champs en sont couverts, ou en marge de bonnes lunettes seules vous protègent les yeux. Les bords de la route sont d'une blancheur crayeuse. A peine la pluie allait-t-elle, ça recommence. Et la pluie ne dure pas. Aujourd'hui arrivée de M. Fox.

L'impeccable M. Fox vient à bicyclette de Caen, maigre, hâve, sans col. Un casque français, peint en bleu, derrière sa bicyclette. Il nous raconte la prise de la ville. St Etienne et le lycée sont encore debout, c'est là que se trouvaient tous les réfugiés. Les Allemands maintenant essayent de les atteindre, l'église a déjà reçu un obus. L'Abbaye aux hommes est intacte aussi. La ville est encore presque inhabitable, constamment sous le feu des allemands et M. Fox nous demande de donner l'hospitalité à sa mère. Grosse canonnade cette nuit —

Lundi 17 juillet

Brouillard et beau temps, le vent est bien placé au Nord. J'aperçois le major Hodgson qui fait sa toilette sur le banc de pierre. A 8h départ pour Bayeux dans la voiture des pionniers. Je vais servir d'interprète à un officier qui veut remettre en état la glacière de la ville près du port. Bien délabrée… Déjeuner au Lion d'Or où je retrouve notre gentil docteur écossais avec

One of the pages of the blue version, July 16th-17th, 1944.

145

Bernard Marze (left) with a monitor.

Blanche Lahaulle, 'my loyal Blanche'.

M. and Mme Marze, with Pat, Marcelle Fauchier Delavigne's dog.

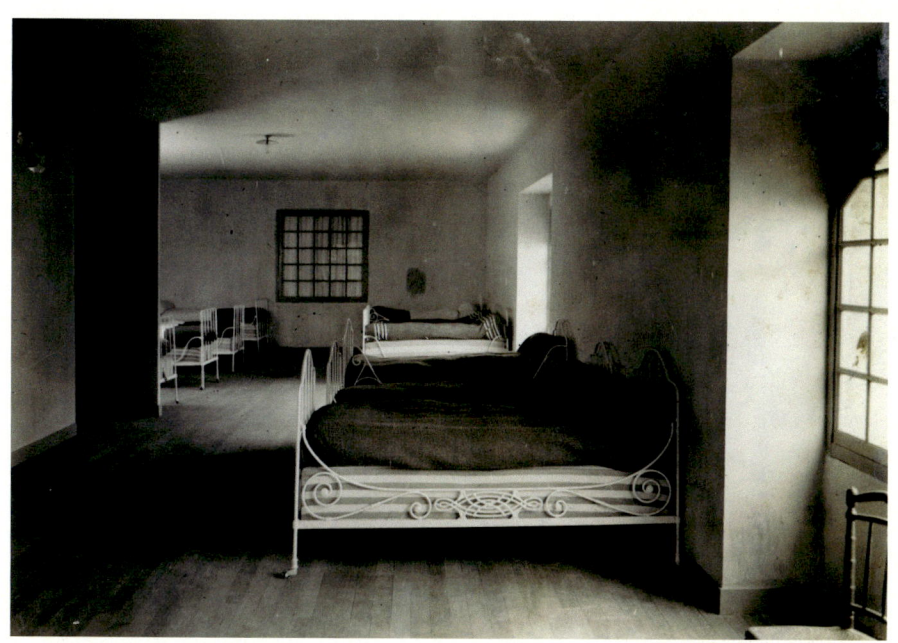

The student dormitory. 'A bombshell just went through the roof over the dormitory.'

The student canteen. 'Then I join everybody else in the canteen.'

Some students of the Garden Centre.

*Student Gavey (also written Gavet, fourth from the left),
who was to have a few altercations with the German occupiers.*

Classes of 1942-1945, with Marcelle Fauchier Delavigne and Bernard Marze.

In 1942.

In 1944.

Emmanuel and Marcelle Fauchier Delavigne (and an unknown friend),
with their grandchildren.

Jean, Marcelle Fauchier Delavigne's son, who died for France in 1940 (the tallest young man on the photograph).

German assault gun from the 352. Infanterie-Division.

*Destroyed Sherman, it was nº 44 of Lieutenant Charlton, from B Squadron,
4th/7th Royal Dragoon Guards.*

Dakota transport plane on the B-6 airfield in Coulombs.

*Example of a 'silver sausage', or barrage balloon. 'Under a threatening sky and hundreds of silver barrage balloons (*saucisses d'argent*) the whole English fleet covers the sea as far as the eye can see.' (D-Day Wings Museum, Bretteville-sur-Odon.)*

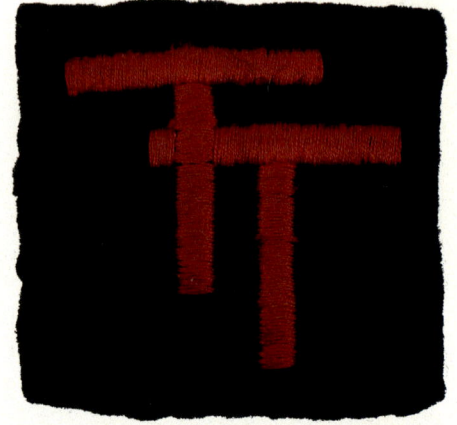

The Tyne and Tees insignia.
'Two Ts on his sleeve, standing
for two rivers, the Tyne and Tees.'

Flags on top of the tower: British,
Russian and American.

Captain Hemming on the garden wall of the Fauchier Delavigne house
(photograph taken by Marcelle).

*Canadians in the priory courtyard, in the company of Mme Marze
(photograph taken by par Marcelle Fauchier Delavigne).*

Rehearsal for the concert organised on Saturday, 24th June 1944.

The geraniums. 'All our best geraniums surround the regimental badge.'

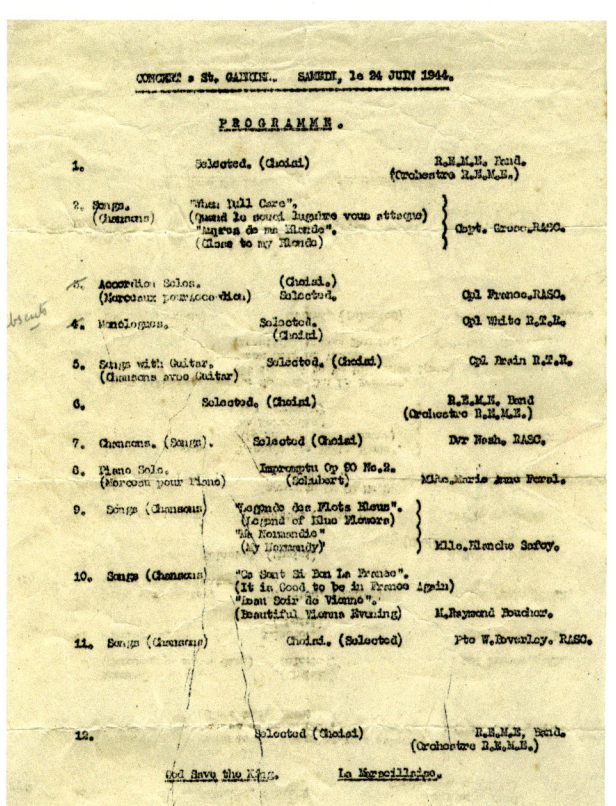

Programme of the concert held on 24th June 1944.

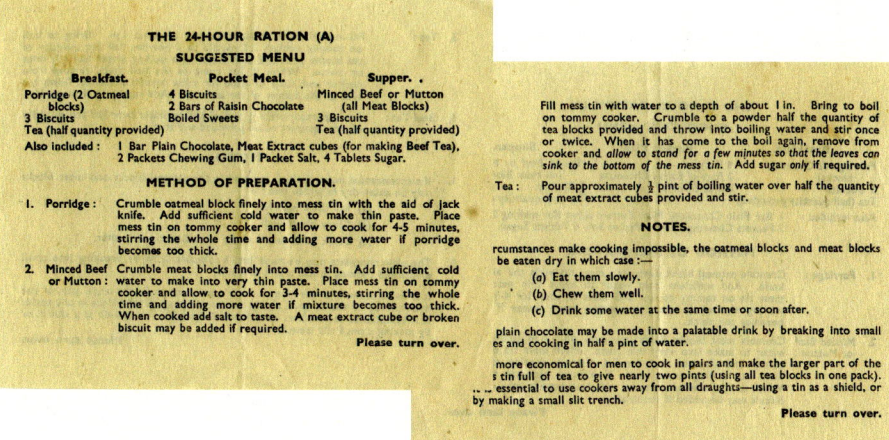

Contents of a British ration (both sides). 'We can understand that with time they grow tired of their monotonous rations.'

A 5-franc 'flagged banknote' (both sides), put into circulation just after D-Day. 'The first note of this new currency with a French flag on it has appeared and enchants me.'

News Bulletin dated 23rd of August 1944 announcing the liberation of Paris.

News Bulletin 1300 hrs Wednesday 23 Aug 44.

The Free French forces of the Interior have liberated PARIS.

240 miles separate the northern and southern forces in France.

General rising decreed by Council of Resistance and Paris Liberation bodies. 50,000 armed members of the F.F.I. and thousands of unarmed compatriots went into the battle. Compatriots in possession of all public buildings. PARIS had been in the hands of the Germans since June 14 1940.

American spearheads 55 miles from LYONS, in the heart of the Rhone valley.
Heavy fighting inside the great naval base of TOULON – ½ mile from the naval arsenal.

Allied forces have liberated SENS.

No confirmation of the Spanish report of a fresh landing in the area of BORDEAUX.

—–ooo000ooo—–

Employment office in Bayeux at 10 rue Saint-Malo.

Marcelle Fauchier Delavigne and Kay Hood.
'She is tall, dark, laughs readily, and is called Miss Hood.'

Marcelle Fauchier Delavigne reading on a windowsill.
'Rest all day in the sun beside the window, reading a little.'

From left to right: Emmanuel Fauchier Delavigne
(with the dog, Pat, in front of him), Kay Hood and
Marcelle Fauchier Delavigne. 'I rush out, excited.
Mano is on the steps! Paris is saved!'

Acknowledgments

Our thanks go to:

Claude Marze, for his childhood memories and providing the two reels of films taken by his uncle, a valuable testimony of D-Day.

Jean-François Le Cuziat, for providing the military information on pages 26, 31, 152, and 153, as well as the photos on pages 152 and 153.

Laurent Lamoureux, for his sketches.

Claude Fauchier Delavigne is a retired teacher whith a Ph.D. in history [her thesis focused on 'The Reinhart family, a Protestant trading family in Le Havre, 1852-1962']. She has coordinated the Saint-Gabriel Priory Cultural Association since 2003, organizing annual exhibitions. She is the author of a brochure on the Saint-Gabriel Priory and co-author of *Secrets de murs*. As an associate member of the Naval Academy, she published *Les pilotes du Havre de 1806 à 1914* and contributed to drafting of extra-curriculars documents.

Julien Crué is qualified historian, a journalist, and a member of the Saint-Gabriel Priory Cultural Association.

TABLE OF CONTENTS

Credits:

Photo album from Marcelle Fauchier Delavigne, courtesy of Hervé and Alain Fauchier Delavigne: cover, pages 146bd, 146bg, 147, 148h, 148b, 149, 150, 151, 154b, 155, 156, 157, 158b, 159b, 160

Marcelle Fauchier Delavigne collection: pages 24, 145, 158h

Photographs taken by M. Léopold Marze, courtesy of Claude et Jean-Jacques Marze: pages 146h, 152, 154g

Coustal collection: page 148 centre

Julien Crué: page 153b

Kay Hood: page 153h

Life collection: page 159b

Imperial War Museum (INS 5131): page 154d

Drawings by Laurent Lamoureux: pages 20, 21, 33, 38, 42, 50

OREP Éditions, Zone tertiaire de Nonant, 14400 BAYEUX
Tel.: 02 31 51 81 31 – Fax: 02 31 51 81 32
E-mail: info@orepeditions.com – Website: www.orepeditions.com
Editor: Grégory PIQUE – Conception: OREP Éditions
Editorial coordination: Sophie LAJOYE
Layout: Antoine SALMON
Translation: Alice POSTEL, Hugo GROSJEAN, Justine DESFRIECHES,
Elisa MAISONNEUVE and Stella GUENERIE - master Traduction Interprétation -
Parcours traduction spécialisée et localisation, université de Caen.

ISBN: 978-2-8151-0889-8
© OREP Éditions 2024